**Turning Point**
Is there hope for broken lives?

To Tanya

with very much
love

Jennifer Rees Larcombe

x

*Also by Jennifer Rees Larcombe*

Beyond Healing
Where Have You Gone, God?
Leaning on a Spider's Web
Unexpected Healing

# Turning Point

## Is there hope for broken lives?

Jennifer Rees Larcombe

Hodder & Stoughton
LONDON SYDNEY AUCKLAND

Acknowledgments for the Bible versions used
in this book can be found on p.vi.

ISBN 0 340 60163 9

Typeset by Hewer Text Composition Services, Edinburgh.

Printed and bound in Great Britain by Cox & Wyman, Reading, Berks.

Hodder and Stoughton Ltd
A Division of Hodder Headline PLC
338 Euston Road
London NW1 3BH

To P. and J., with grateful thanks
for teaching me how to forgive.
Without your help, I could not have
written this book.

# CONTENTS

# FOREWORD

We are delighted to commend Jen's latest book, which answers so many of life's questions in such a humorous, compassionate and sensible way.

We all face bereavement in more ways than we probably realise – not only through the death of a loved one. We can go through the same emotions when we lose our car keys or wave goodbye to our daughter on her first day at school! We often feel riddled with guilt because we are not meeting other people's expectations of our behaviour at any given time. This book sets the record straight by enabling us to understand and face the emotions we are experiencing.

Paul wrote to the Corinthians: 'What a wonderful God we have – he is the Father of our Lord Jesus Christ, the source of every mercy, and the one who so wonderfully comforts and strengthens us in our hardships and trials. And why does he do this? So that when others are troubled, needing our sympathy and encouragement, we can pass on to them this same help and comfort God has given us' (2 Cor. 1:3–4, LB).

Jen has learnt these lessons in the school of life, sometimes through almost intolerable circumstances. We are grateful to her for passing on these lessons and we are confident they will be a blessing to every reader.

*Roy and Fiona Castle*

# PREFACE

This is a book for those who boil with anger behind smiles that say, 'I'm all right, everything's fine.' It is for people who are full of those questions that Christians aren't supposed to ask, and doubts that would shock their friends at church – if only they knew about them, it's for those who wake at five in the morning and start on a 'What if . . . ?' cycle – 'What if I can't cope . . . ? What if the money runs out . . . ? What if I never get better?' It's a book for the person who is convinced that he or she must be the only Christian who feels depressed, or for extroverts who can sit smiling broadly in the middle of a room full of people – and yet feel so lonely that they wish they were dead. Feeling broken like this inside is horrible. I know, because I once felt like that myself.

Lives can be shattered and dreams destroyed for all kinds of reasons. Sometimes it happens through large, dramatic events, but just as often people experience a gradual and secret realisation that they are not now the people they used to be or hoped they might become. We can be 'broken' by someone else, or our lives can be smashed by our own mistakes, but often there seems to be no one specific to blame – except God himself. Whatever or whoever caused it all, the sense of inner brokenness is devastating, and we begin to fear that our lives will be like this for ever.

I believe we *can* be mended – I certainly was, and I have seen too many other lives remade to doubt that it can happen. The mending process takes time; it cannot be rushed. But for me there was a definite turning point, a moment when my lost hope began to be restored and the tide turned. I have come to believe that this turning point is the key to rebuilding broken lives, and so I decided to write this book. It comes to you with my love and prayers, and I hope it will feel personal – the hand of a friend reaching out in the darkness.

Most of the chapters in this book offer tips and strategies which I have found personally helpful when coping with all the odd feelings of anger, fear, confusion and despair which seem to hit most of us after some kind of major loss. The chapters finish with a meditation or a story from the Bible which has helped me, and a prayer

I would like to thank the people I mention in the book for kindly allowing me to do so. They are all real people, but to spare them any embarrassment I have changed their names and some of the minor details of their stories. Most of all, I should like to thank a remarkable bunch of people, all of whom have discovered this mysterious 'turning point' in their own lives. They gave me their promise to pray every day as I worked on the manuscript, and I have constantly felt the power of their prayers over the last few months. This book comes to you with their love, too, and they have prayed for you already, many times over. They are some of the most amazing people I know, yet many never leave their homes because of disability or chronic illness – and all have gone through deep personal suffering. Perhaps the rest of the world might not think they were powerful, but they most certainly are! Their power comes from their unshakeable belief in God and his ability to mend broken people.

> *There is hope for a tree that has been cut down; it can come back to life and sprout. Even though its roots grow old, and its stump dies in the ground, with water it will sprout like a young plant.* (Job 14:7–9, GNB)

# ACKNOWLEDGMENTS

Many thanks to Dr Jenny Brown for all her help concerning medical details; to Dr Sarah Williams for her advice; to Cath Isaaks and the Burrswood Counselling Team; to George and Yvonne Adams; and to Murray Gabriel – who had the worst job of all: correcting my spelling mistakes. Most of all, thanks to Tony and our children, who put up with burnt dinners for many months while my mind was on other things.

# 1

# THE DAY THE TEAPOT WAS BROKEN

My granny had a teapot. It was no ordinary teapot. In fact, it was far too precious to be used at all – except on Christmas Day. For the rest of the year it stood in isolated splendour behind the glass doors of her display cabinet. 'A thing of beauty is a joy for ever,' she would tell me as I squashed my nose up against the diamond panes and gazed at it in awe. 'That teapot belonged to your great-great-grandmother,' she would add, using the reverent whisper she generally reserved for church. 'It's very valuable. It's my little nest egg – so I won't be a burden to anyone when I'm old. If anything goes wrong I can always sell the teapot.' To me, she was old already, and we all knew she would never sell the teapot – whatever happened. If the house caught fire, I am sure she would have rescued her precious antique before she even considered saving herself.

Then one Christmas a dreadful thing happened. At first it was just like any other Christmas. All the members of the family were gathered at Granny's house by midday, and the Christmas dinner tasted just as wonderful as usual. The only slight hitch came after the pudding had been carried in, blazing with blue brandy flames. Everyone was enjoying their share when an anguished cry from my small brother managed to turn sixteen startled faces in his direction. He had swallowed the shilling piece, which was always hidden somewhere among the currants and raisins. He was convinced he would die at any moment, but it seemed to be the loss of a whole shilling that *really* worried him!

By three o'clock, however, he had forgotten all about it as we squashed into the front room to hear the King on the BBC Home Service. In those days people still stood up for the national anthem – even after a large Christmas dinner. Then came the ceremonial opening of the presents while Grandpa puffed his way through one of the fat Havana cigars we always gave him in a sandalwood box. By this time, the crackling fire had raised the temperature in the crowded little room to sauna proportions.

'I'm getting very dry, my dears,' said Granny. 'Let's have some tea.' It was probably the last beverage anyone fancied just then, but we knew she needed an excuse for the teapot's annual ceremonial appearance.

It was while we were all milling about in the kitchen after tea that the fatal accident happened. I can't remember which of my uncles dropped the teapot, but the crash cut a horrified silence right across all the happy noises in the house. 'If only you could turn the hands of a clock backwards,' was my instinctive thought. 'Then it wouldn't have to happen.'

My granny had hard, red, quarry tiles on her back kitchen floor. I remember standing looking down at the pieces of teapot, scattered in all directions over the shiny surface – sharp, jagged, painful pieces surrounding a pathetic heap of soggy tea leaves. Then I looked up at Granny's face, and I will never forget her expression. Something precious, beautiful and irreplaceable had gone for ever. The future was no longer safely insured, and a lifeline to the past had been severed.

Somehow that moment stuck in my memory. All the characters in the scene were left suspended in time, like a video put on hold. Years later, it all came back to me as I lay in a hospital bed in London. Once again I felt the same sickening devastation as I realised that my life had been smashed, just like the teapot, and the pieces lay in fragments around me. I had been seriously ill, and the doctors were not at all sure that I would ever make a full recovery.*

'You are very lucky to survive,' the nurses told me. 'Lots of people die from what you had.' I was not so sure I was lucky when I realised that the illness had left me handicapped in many ways. 'How will I ever cope when I get home?' I thought miserably, when I found I couldn't even stand up without the floor jumping up to hit me, and I slurped tea all over the bed because my hands refused to grip the cup. 'I can't even look after myself properly, so how on earth will I manage the children?' When I tried to tell people how I felt, my words often jumbled themselves up into a hopeless mess that no one could understand. Worst of all, a catheter bag stood waiting to trip up my visitors every time they approached the bed. Would life, trapped in a body like this, be worth living?

* I have described this more fully in *Beyond Healing* and *Unexpected Healing*.

It had all seemed so perfect – before. We had six children, the youngest was only four years old and all of them were healthy and happy. We had just finished doing up our dream house in the country, and the garden was well stocked and neatly planted with vegetables and fruit. We had been living out the ideal existence we had always longed to achieve, but when I began to realise that the self-sufficient 'good life' in the country would be impossible now I was disabled, I felt as if our happiness had been smashed for ever – just like Granny's beautiful teapot. All our dreams and hopes seemed to lie around me in sharp, scattered pieces – how would I ever get them all back together again?

I know now that this sense of personal devastation is far more common than I realised then. I frequently meet people these days who say, for all kinds of reasons, 'My life just seems to have fallen apart.' The statement sounds like a cliché, but I cannot think of a better way of describing how it actually feels.

## Some 'Teapots' Break Suddenly

Sometimes the crash comes suddenly and dramatically. Perhaps you open the front door to two policemen who tell you that your husband has died on his way home from work. Or, the hospital consultant may say, 'I'm afraid it's cancer.' Or: 'Sorry, but you're redundant,' your employer announces. Or perhaps you find a note from your wife telling you she has gone to live with someone else – and she's taken the children with her.

## Some 'Teapots' Break Gradually

Sometimes the pieces fall apart more slowly. You find it hard to remember the exact moment when you realised that the relationship you thought was going to be permanent was beginning to crack and split; when the friends at church you loved and trusted began to turn against you; when you first noticed the 'clay feet' of the person you admired, relied on and trusted completely. Or you can't pinpoint exactly when the healthy body that had always obeyed you began to let you down. Perhaps the 'teapot' took so long to fall to the floor that all you can really be sure about is the fact that it is certainly broken now.

## Some 'Teapots' Are Only Made of Dreams

Some 'teapots' never actually existed outside of your own dreams and hopes – but that does not make the moment you recognised their loss any less agonising. It is possible to wake up one morning to the fact that you will never now be the person you always intended to be: the goals you set for your life were unattainable after all.

When Marion left Bible college, she would have gone anywhere for God. She was willing to evangelise the world like Billy Graham, or care for the poor like Mother Teresa. Ten years later, her life had narrowed to the confines of a suburban flat and the needs of three small children. She was overweight, unhappily married, and spiritually smothered by a boring church.

Shelley had always hoped that 'when she grew up' she would throw off her shy, retiring nature and develop the kind of sparkling personality that would draw other people to her like a magnet. At forty-five, it suddenly dawned on her that she was still on the outside of any group, marginalised, and usually ignored. The career she had hoped for had never quite happened, and now her life consisted of caring for her elderly mother, struggling with a dull office job, and babysitting for her sister's children.

Gill was about the same age when she finally realised her marriage was never going to be as romantic and tender as she had been convinced it would be on her wedding day. In fact, it had turned sour – and she was living with a husband who had even stopped trying to pretend that he loved her. The children she had hoped would take Cambridge by storm had turned into monsters who refused to work at school, and who made life unbearable for her at home.

Shattered dreams can be every bit as painful as shattered reality.


## Some 'Teapots' Broke Long Ago

Other 'teapots' have been broken right back in childhood. Often I meet people who go through life feeling 'broken inside – not quite a complete human being'.

'I've always felt like that,' said Mary. 'I don't know why. I can't seem to remember great chunks of my childhood – they're lost in a kind of grey misery. I'm afraid it has something to do with things my father used to do to me, but I can't bring myself to remember them. I don't *want* to remember them. But if I'm honest, I know that whatever was done to me during those grey patches has left me unable to be a normal woman, to marry, to relate to men – even to have the confidence to get the kind of job I know I am capable of doing. Yes, I suppose I've always felt worthless, no good to anyone, broken on the inside.'

Sometimes it is not abuse in childhood that breaks the 'teapot', but some kind of severe loss. As these children grow up, they often try to bury their distress and deny the painful effects of it; but until their grief is acknowledged and dealt with, they are left with a broken 'teapot' inside, lying unmended in painful pieces.

Most of us can fool the outside world quite successfully. We wear a bright smile that says, 'I'm coping, I'm fine,' but inside we feel as if our lives, our dreams, our personalities and our relationships are all lying in little jagged pieces on a red-tiled kitchen floor. As we stand surrounded by the ruins, we probably wish that the hands of the clock could be turned backwards.

### 'You'll Just Have to Come to Terms with It'

I remember a chirpy little student nurse saying that to me as I lay there in the hospital bed. I could have hit her. She was only trying to be helpful, but I thought, 'What does she know about it anyway?' People who have never had their 'teapots' broken trot out that irritating little phrase so glibly. 'You'll just have to accept the new situation and learn to live with it.' It sounds so easy – until you try it! How can we come to terms with something utterly horrible? After all, who wants to be trapped for life in a body that no longer functions properly? Who wants to live alone grieving for the one and only person who made life bearable? Who wants to sit at home all day, pushed out, forgotten and useless? Accepting that life is now irrevocably different is perhaps one of the hardest things that a human being ever has to do. We do not *want* to come to terms with this new kind of life – all we want is the old one back!

'You can do anything if you try hard enough.' That was something Granny often used to say. Probably the first thing she thought after her teapot was broken that Christmas afternoon was, 'I can soon mend it.' After the gasp of horror and the pungent silence in the kitchen, I remember the culprit uncle scrabbling round the floor on hands and knees scooping up all the pieces he could find: his neck purple with embarrassment as it bulged over the collar of his best white shirt.

Outside the back door in the icy darkness stood the dustbin, its lid frosted just like the Christmas cake. It was full of turkey legs, bits of cracker, tight balls of wrapping paper, and cold Brussels sprouts. My uncle began to hurl the bits of teapot in on top, until my grandmother's indignant voice halted him from the open doorway.

'Whatever are you doing?' she demanded. 'You can't throw it away!'

'Mother, that teapot will never hold tea again,' he said firmly, as half the spout went into the bin.

She simply refused to accept such a terrible thought. 'Anything can be mended,' she declared and, pushing past him, began snatching the pieces from among the greasy debris, collecting them carefully in her apron. I can't remember what happened after that, so I guess my parents must have deemed it tactful for us to leave rather hastily.

'This *can't* happen to me!' is how most of us initially feel when something dreadful happens, and it is usually only much later that we begin to realise that the damage is irreversible. We then either accept the situation or are destroyed by it.

Perhaps I should say right now that I did not cope very well with this business of 'coming to terms with it'. In fact, looking back on those first two years of my illness, I can see just what a mess I made of it. It was not living with constant pain and fatigue that got me down, nor was it my disabilities and the restrictions of my life. What really floored me was the way I reacted to it all. A whole range of bewildering emotions that were quite out of character kept taking me by surprise, and caused me to say and do things I heartily regretted.

## Why All the Secrecy?

If only someone had told me that *everyone* feels like that when their 'teapots' are broken. No one warned me that I would feel so angry. No one said that depression is normal after severe loss, so when despair almost drove me to take my own life I thought I must be going mad. No one explained that I might feel like shrivelling up with guilt at the suspicion that it could all be my fault, or that it is common for people to argue and bargain with God – and ask 'Why?' a thousand times a day. When I floated through life, cut off from other people in my own separate bubble of space, I had no idea that this sense of isolation and loneliness is par for the course. These reactions take nearly all of us entirely by surprise, but somehow they have to be lived through *before* we can reach that moment when we can honestly say, 'I have accepted my life the way it is now.'

People try to hurry us to that point of acceptance because we are so hard to live with before we reach it – well, I certainly was! Many of my Christian friends looked askance at my angry outbursts or were shocked by my depression.

'Where's your faith?' they said. 'You ought to be praising the Lord instead of being so negative all the time.' I knew I was behaving badly – lashing out at everyone in sight – but I felt as if my life, as I had known it, was being hurled into the dustbin, just like Granny's teapot, 'never to hold tea again'. I simply did not know how to cope with all the unexpected feelings and reactions that kept on building up inside me. Now, looking back at myself struggling along that lonely road towards adjustment, I can see how much it would have helped to know someone else who had 'been there', and to discover from them some of the things that helped speed their journey. I hope this book will be a 'personal contact' for others who are travelling along behind me.

There is another reason why I wanted to write this book. Two years after I was first rushed into hospital, we reached a terrible time where everything seemed to be going wrong. Not only was I still constantly ill and in pain, but our marriage seemed to be falling apart. I couldn't cope with the children because insecurity made them all so difficult to manage, and we were just about to move from our home in the country. I just did not know where I fitted into the world any longer, or what was going to happen next. At this lowest point of all, something very remarkable happened that transformed the whole scenario for all of us. It was not a great dramatic miracle of instant healing; instead, it was something that can happen to anyone and everyone who wants it. But before I tell you about it, I must finish the story of Granny's teapot.

### The Mended Teapot

After our hasty departure on that fateful Christmas afternoon, I did not see Granny for a number of months. I often thought about her, and wondered if she would manage to glue all the bits of her teapot back together again with her tube of thick brown glue. It was the following July before I went back to see her again, and the first thing

I did was to dash straight into the dining-room. Pressing my nose flat against the doors of the glass cabinet, I looked for the teapot. It wasn't there. Only a dark circle where the velvet had not faded showed where it had once stood so proudly. Poor Granny, I thought. She had failed.

Sadly, I turned round, and there on the window ledge in the sunshine I saw it – what was left of it, anyway. Obviously, she had not managed to find all the pieces: most of the spout was missing, as was the lid, and the handle looked very odd. Like an excavated Egyptian vase in a museum, the teapot was full of little jagged holes and cracks. But Granny had 'green fingers'. She could make anything grow – anywhere. She had filled the carcass of the teapot with rich compost, and out of those holes grew all kinds of beautiful little plants and flowers. Miniature ferns and variegated ivy poked their way out of the gaps, and a begonia with tiny orange flowers cascaded from the hole where the lid should have been, reminding me of soap bubbles escaping from an over-filled washing-machine. The teapot looked so lovely that it took my breath away.

'It's not the same; it never will be,' said Granny, coming up behind me. 'But everyone who comes to see me these days tells me how lovely it looks. I always used to say, "A thing of beauty is a joy for ever",' she added thoughtfully, 'and I suppose it *is* still beautiful, but in a different sort of way.'

---

*God can do wonders with a broken heart so long as you give him all the pieces.* (Victor Alfsen)

# 2

# INSIDE THE BROKEN TEAPOT

My granny's broken teapot had a happy ending, but not all the stories of broken lives finish quite so well. Some 'teapots' take years to mend, and others stay in fragments for ever.

How is it that some people seem able to adapt to massive trauma and upheaval and, like Granny's teapot, allow their lives to be reshaped and given a new purpose? Other people experience similar tragedy, but they leave the broken pieces in the dustbin and give up on life completely, while their friends say gloomily, 'How sad, he never got over it.'

Why do some people gather up the pieces and hold them tightly, as if the jagged shards were some kind of comfort? These little fragments of the past are all they have to cling to now. In fact, they become so absorbed in them that they never consider that the future is also there, waiting to be lived.

Others collect the broken pieces and arrange them carefully in the display cabinet as a perpetual reproach to the person they blame for the disaster. Being 'a broken person' becomes a way of life. They show the fragments off to everyone who comes near them, endlessly requiring pity, and gaining comfort (and even importance) from the attention.

There are probably hundreds of reasons for staying in pieces, but I believe there is a way that broken lives can be mended. It happened like this for me. It was two years after I first became ill that I reached that 'all time low' that I mentioned in the last chapter. It was one

*The Lord is near to those who are discouraged; he saves those who have lost all hope.* (Ps. 34:18, GNB)

Saturday morning just before we were due to move from our home in the country. The children were all being diabolical, my pain level was uncomfortably high, and the house seemed full of packing cases that tripped us up or ripped our clothes with their sharp metal corners. Tony made some bright but irritating comment that triggered off a major row, and suddenly all I wanted to do was go away by myself and scream very loudly indeed. 'Everything had got on top of me' may be yet another cliché, but it describes exactly that feeling of being weighed down and crushed by problems that no one seems able to solve.

Struggling out of the house on my elbow crutches, I fell over, face down, in a lake of manure at the bottom of our garden.* I struggled in the dung, vainly trying to get myself back on to the grass, but my arms and legs were not strong enough. I felt as if the manure was sucking me down, and in the end I simply had to give up and sit still until someone came along to pull me out.

I was crying with rage, not only at the indignity of being stuck in that ghastly mess, but at the frustration of being trapped in a similar way by my problems. I wanted to vent all my fury on the person who had disintegrated my nice, well-organised life, and turned it into a mass of stinking muck – but who was really to blame? I had been so angry with Tony that morning that I had thrown the steam iron at him, but it was not his fault that I was ill. Nor were the doctors at fault because they could not cure me. My friends irritated me with their tactless advice, and the children drove me up the wall with their bad behaviour. I was angry with all these people, but suddenly I realised who I was really holding responsible . . .

## It Was God Himself

Lying in the muck, I told God what I thought of him for allowing me to become ill in the first place, and then refusing to hear all those prayers for healing. I was so abusive that I deserved to be struck

* See *Unexpected Healing*, p. 93.

> *God has blocked the way, and I can't get through; he has hidden my path in darkness.* (Job 19:8, GNB)

down by lightning, but instead I really believe he answered me. These words formed themselves inside my head: 'I know about the mess, but I want to be in the centre of all those problems with you, and I would be, if only you would let me.' As I lay there in all that filth, I felt utterly overwhelmed by his love – it really was the most amazing experience of my life! Gradually I began to realise that for months I had been blaming God for everything that had been going wrong. By holding all these grudges against him, I had pushed him out of the centre of my life and allowed the problems and worries to take his place.

It was a long time before anyone came to find me. Somehow, as I sat there, I kept on thinking of Granny pulling the pieces of broken teapot out from among the rubbish and carefully collecting them in her apron. I found myself giving God the fragments of my life one by one – the broken body, the broken dreams and hopes, the broken marriage and family security, and – most of all – the broken faith in his goodness and care. I asked him to come into the middle of the mess my life had become, to take control of it, and to mend it for me.

I believe he did that. I did not feel any different at the time, but a few weeks later I was aware that something had definitely happened. It was not that the circumstances of my life suddenly became easier; it was the way I felt about those circumstances that had changed.

It was 'letting go' of the past and of my hidden resentment against God that made room for him to come back into the central place and begin to mend me from the inside. He did not put me back together in the way I would have expected, but he did allow new things to 'grow' out of the broken places. In the past, my happiness had come from outward things such as good health, a perfect home, and an identity in the village community; so that when they were lost, my happiness went too. Having God in the centre gave me a new kind of inner happiness that has nothing to do with the outside circumstances of life. It is a supernatural peace and joy that goes on bubbling away internally – however difficult the outside circumstances may be.

Soon the rest of the family caught this 'peacejoy' too, and the children settled happily into our new home and our marriage became stronger than ever before. I had the time to write books and speak

*He heals the broken-hearted and bandages their wounds.*
(Ps. 147:3, GNB)

from my wheelchair in churches and Christian meetings, and the very fact that I was always at home made it possible for other hurting people to stop by for a chat. I was no better physically, and in fact my health deteriorated drastically over the next six years, but I think God mended my 'teapot' all the same. Being ill had not finished my life – it had simply changed its shape.

I always seem to see things in pictures, and this is the way I visualise what happened to me after falling in the cow dung. The following diagrams show what I was like during those first two years of my illness. God was there, but pushed right out on the edges of my life. The problems filled the centre and dominated my thinking.

When I asked God to come into the centre of my life, his love began to push the problems out to the edges, making them seem so much less important. They were still there, but they no longer obsessed my thinking and defeated me. The more I allowed God to pour his love into me, the more he could do to help and mend me.

## That Vital Moment of Letting Go

I have often tried to picture my granny sitting at her kitchen table, carefully trying to glue all those bits of china back together again. How did she feel when she first realised that she had not managed to find all the pieces in the dustbin? Did she wonder if it was worth continuing with the intricate repairing job if her precious teapot could never be perfect again? Did there come a moment when she let go her memory of the teapot as it had been, and began to picture it in a new shape?

How did she feel about the person who dropped it? I know she was furious with him at first, because her ears always turned red when she was angry. Did she ever consider making him feel guilty by displaying the wreckage in her cabinet? Perhaps she did, but later she must have decided to set aside her resentment, or she could never have lavished so much loving care on reshaping her treasure.

The more I think about it, the more convinced I am that this 'letting go' of what is past, and also of the person responsible for the 'breakage', is the key to rebuilding broken lives.

## Who Is Responsible?

'Teapots' do not break all by themselves – we can always find someone to blame.

God says, 'The mountains and hills may crumble, but my love for you will never end; I will keep for ever my promise of peace.' (Isa. 54:10, GNB)

- Sometimes the culprit is obvious – the husband who walked out, the boss who gave us the sack, the father who abused us – or perhaps a whole chain of people contributed to our misery.
- Sometimes we only have ourselves to blame for the mess we are in, yet oddly it can be harder to forgive ourselves than anyone else!
- When the answer is not so obvious we often blame God – just as I did. 'If he really loved me and had the power the Bible says he has, then he would have healed me,' was my unvoiced accusation.

To forgive means to give up a grudge and to stop blaming someone. Being willing to do that for the person who 'broke our teapot' seems, in some mysterious way, to set us free to live again.

### 'But Forgiving a Man Like Him Is Quite Impossible'

'Everyone I meet keeps on telling me I must forgive him!' Those were the words of a friend of mine, Fiona, and they were said to me some years ago. 'They make me mad! It's easy to spout on about forgiving and letting go of the past when you've never been hurt badly yourself! If they were married to someone like him, they'd find forgiving impossible too!'

Since then, I have met many other people who feel the same as Fiona, and I believe she was right: forgiving is impossible when someone has devastated your life and damaged the people you love. Yet her life stayed in ruins until she had forgiven her husband. So how did she manage to do the impossible?

#### She had to get help from outside

Back in the days when I was surrounded by umpteen screaming babies and toddlers in temper tantrums, I was asked to a coffee morning talk entitled 'Anger in the Family'. I thought it might do me good! It was there I met Fiona.

---

*Everyone says forgiveness is a lovely idea until they have something to forgive.* (C.S. Lewis)

Before the official proceedings began, we chatted as we munched homemade biscuits, and she told me she had been a Christian for ten years and went to a church on the other side of town. Our children were all about the same age, and we were getting on so well that I felt mildly irritated when the speaker began her talk. My irritation did not fade either as she told us about her two perfect daughters, both away at boarding school, and her husband – who seemed to have a highly paid job and a positively saint-like disposition. As I listened, I felt that even *I* could keep my temper in such idyllic circumstances. Towards the end of the talk the speaker began to talk about forgiveness, and suddenly I felt a volcanic eruption in the seat beside me. With a snort of disgust, Fiona leapt to her feet and sent her chair crashing into the lap of an astonished-looking lady in a pink velvet hat. Everyone in the room looked on aghast as Fiona stormed out of the room, banging the door behind her. I slid out in her wake because I had noticed the distress in her face, and was just in time to see her disappearing upstairs to the crèche in one of the bedrooms. I caught up with her on the landing, and she turned on me like a cornered animal.

'Leave me alone!' She almost spat the words at me. 'You lot make me sick! All happily married, well off, smug little Christians. And yet you tell me to forgive!'

'I'm sorry,' I said nervously, 'But p'raps if you explained . . . ?'

'He doesn't even *want* to be forgiven – he's telling everyone it's my fault we broke up. He's spreading the most amazing lies just to put himself in a better light. I must have been blind – or thick! It had all been going on for months before I twigged – she even went to our church! We were in the same housegroup; she was my *friend*! I just don't know how they could . . .'

'What's happening now?' I ventured.

'He wants a divorce, but my kids cry for their daddy every night. Their security's shot to bits because we've got to move – he wants to sell the house so he can use his share to set up home with her! They'll have to change schools and, worst of all, I'll be out at work full time unless he gives us more money. How could he do all that to his own

---

*He pulled me out of a dangerous pit, out of the deadly quicksand. He set me safely on a rock and made me secure.* (Ps. 40:2, GNB)

kids? And yet everyone seems to imply I'm the wicked one because I can't forgive.'

By that time, the meeting below must have finished because up the stairs behind us surged the speaker and the lady of the house. They obviously knew Fiona and her circumstances well. I could hardly believe my ears when the speaker said sweetly, 'My dear, you really must forgive and forget. Why don't we have a little prayer together?'

Fiona's response is best forgotten, but sadly she is typical of so many who are urged into making some kind of mental assent or verbal statement far too soon. Just to keep everyone happy they comply, but real forgiveness does not happen in the head; it comes from the heart, and when nothing inside seems to change they feel they have failed.

Fiona, like everyone else, needed to feel the pain first, express the anger, grieve the loss, and experience the sorrow before she was ready to face the issue of forgiveness. She was afraid to come too close to God because she thought he too would force her to forgive. First she simply needed to talk. Then, gradually, over many months, she began to turn back to God again and open herself up to his love, rather as I did in the cow dung. One morning she was finally ready to be made willing to forgive. The following week, when I popped in to see her, I found this little prayer pinned on her kitchen wall: 'Lord, I can't forgive them, but please put your love in my heart and forgive them for me. And please forgive me for not being able to forgive.'

Now, years later, her children have left home and she is in charge of a small private nursing home. She loves her job, and in her spare time is heavily involved in her church's activities. Her 'teapot' is certainly mended, and I asked her, 'Did you find it easy to forgive in the end?'

'No way!' she replied vehemently. 'It's taken me years – and even now I can't be quite *sure* I have forgiven entirely. I think it's something you have to keep on working at – for ever. But life changed for me the moment I decided to spit out the hate, and breathe

---

*Forgiveness is not a sweet, platonic ideal to be dispensed to the world like perfume sprayed from a fragrance bottle. It is an unnatural act which is blatantly unfair and achingly difficult. Long after you have forgiven, the wound lives on in the memory.* (Philip Yancey)

in the love of Jesus. I've had to do the same thing millions of times since, because the resentments and angry feelings keep coming back in waves, but every time I "spit out and breathe in", I feel better. I still think it would have been impossible for me to forgive on my own. I needed Jesus to forgive through me, and then of course he was able to heal all the damage those two did to me and the children. In fact, despite everything, I'm really pleased with how well the children have turned out!'

'Would you mind if I wrote about what happened to you?' I asked her.

'Not now, I wouldn't,' she replied, 'now I'm mended. But do tell people they *must* be willing to allow God to "do it *his* way". He must be the boss. He has to be in complete control of everything if we want him to mend us. Otherwise, he's limited like a back-seat driver who can't help much in an emergency. He has to sit in the driver's seat and take the wheel before he can control a skid or avoid a crash. And,' she added finally, 'tell them that forgiving takes time, even with God's help!'

Perhaps, like Fiona, you feel you are being pressurised by others into making a hasty decision to forgive before you are really ready. If so, it might be better to put the whole subject on the 'back burner' while you read the rest of this book. Towards the end of the book there are some practical tips on letting go which you may find helpful.

God's Presence

'There's no one I can really blame for what's happened to me, and how can God mend me when I don't feel he's there any more?' If you are feeling like that, it may be a help to know that many other people feel the same. Experts agree that one of the results of shock and intolerable stress is a complete loss of the feeling of God's presence. So whether you feel his presence or not, it does not alter the fact that he *is* there and he *can* help you. You simply have to make the decision to ask God to mend your life. The rest is up to him.

> *He who cannot forgive others breaks the bridge over which he must pass himself. For every man has need to be forgiven.* (George Herbert)

## But It Can't Be That Easy!

You're dead right. It isn't that easy – even with God's help – and when I fell in the cow dung, I would have lashed out at anyone who suggested that it was.

When my granny pulled the bits of teapot out of the dustbin, she was only just *beginning* her repairing job – not finishing it. The process of mending and adjustment usually takes a lot longer than most of us think that it should! Human beings cannot adapt suddenly to massive changes without all kinds of unexpected and disconcerting side effects, even with God in the driver's seat of their lives. As I said in the last chapter, some of these reactions can be most embarrassing, particularly for people who want to live the Christian life.

Everyone in the village loved Martin. He had been their vicar for twenty-seven years. 'He's got a big round red smile, and he laughs so much that he bounces when he walks.' That was the way one six-year-old member of his congregation described him in the parish magazine, and most people felt it was an apt description. Yet when Martin's wife died after a long and agonising illness, he lost his 'round red smile' completely for a while and shut himself away in the vicarage study.

'I've helped so many people through bereavement over the years,' he told his brother-in-law, who was also a clergyman, 'but I never thought it actually felt like this. Surely a man who has served the Lord for as many years as I have shouldn't feel depressed like this. And the anger!' His parishioners were surprised too.

'Fancy the vicar behaving like that!' said the postmistress. 'He snapped my head off the other day, and he couldn't be bothered to visit my auntie in hospital. You'd have thought his faith would have meant more to him than that, wouldn't you?'

Martin was not suffering from some deep spiritual problem: he was actually behaving like a normal human being going through what the experts call 'the grieving process'. Such experts devise diagrams to show us what to expect, and they make it look as if it is all a well-charted journey through clearly defined stages:

---

*What wound did heal but by degrees*? (William Shakespeare)

---

- shock
  - denial
    - recognition
      - anger
        - fear – anxiety
          - guilt
            - despair – depression
              - isolation – loneliness
                - questioning – bargaining
                  - and finally, acceptance

However, people are all different. We don't all move through the process from one nice neat stage to another in an orderly sequence. Some people start in the middle and finish near the beginning, while others do the whole thing backwards. In fact, it can feel more like a crazy game of snakes and ladders when our emotions send us zooming up and down and back and forth with quite remarkable rapidity. Some people even say they feel as if they are experiencing several of the emotions all at once! We just have to keep on reminding ourselves that the process is different for each of us, and we all travel through it at our own individual pace.

## *Warning!*

There is nothing tidy and systematic about this process that I have christened the 'Broken Teapot Syndrome'! So don't feel you have to wade through this book chronologically. If you are full of questions and plagued by endless 'whys?', turn straight to Chapter 8. If you are so angry you feel like a walking volcano ready to flare up at anyone who comes too close, take a look at Chapter 9. Just let the book scratch you where you itch most!

---

*Jesus said, 'He has sent me to . . . deliver those who are oppressed . . . downtrodden, bruised, crushed and broken down by calamity.'* (Luke 4:18, AMP)

### The Puzzled Spectators

The rest of the world sits around and watches us playing this weird game of snakes and ladders, but few of them understand what we are going through.

'If someone in my family had died, I think people would find it easier to understand why I keep crying,' said Rhianan, who had just had her leg amputated. She was right; everyone would have rallied round to support her through a bereavement, but few understand that other losses can feel almost as bad. It is possible to grieve for a job, health, ministry, reputation, marriage, friend, money or a home.

### A Secret Kind of Grief

Amanda lost both her parents in a car accident when she was only five, yet she appeared to grow up quite unaffected by the loss. Then, when she was thirty-five, she lost her job. It was only a minor tragedy in comparison with her childhood experience, but somehow it triggered off the memories she had buried and they all came surging to the surface. She went through the whole grieving process just as if her trauma had happened yesterday. It seemed ridiculous to admit she was crying for a mother she lost thirty years before, so instead of having the support and sympathy that people receive when they are 'publicly' bereaved, she had to suffer in secret.

Grieving for the loss of broken dreams and shattered hopes is just as embarrassing and quite as painful. Because this kind of pain is harder to acknowledge or express, people going through these secret crises can become so agitated internally that they may go into a depression and even suffer a complete breakdown.

### Why Is It Harder for Christians?

Secular 'experts' tell us that all our muddled emotions are perfectly normal, but we find it difficult to cope with them because we think:

> *Forgiveness is the key which unlocks the door of resentment and the handcuffs of hatred. It breaks the chains of bitterness and the shackles of selfishness.* (Corrie ten Boom)

- Christians should be tranquil and accepting, not angry.
- Christians should trust God, not keep on asking 'why?'
- Christians should be full of joy and triumph, not depression.
- Christians should be outgoing, not isolated and lonely.
- Christians shouldn't worry: they should praise God – and sing hymns loudly!
- Christians shouldn't always feel guilty, because Jesus died for them.

So we push these awkward feelings down behind a 'bright Christian smile' and deny their existence – even to ourselves. Christians, though, are human beings, not robots or angels, and human beings happen to feel all this and far more when their 'teapots' are broken. Later in the book it might be good to look at some of these emotions and discover ways of coping with them, and even how they can be turned around and used creatively to our advantage.

Although Christians can feel as devastated as anyone else by personal disaster, we have one huge advantage: we do not have to face the misery of it all on our own. Yet there have been times when I've felt so badly hurt that it was hard to accept that truth, so it has always been a great relief to me to know that one of the greatest 'saints' in history also found it difficult.

---

## A Meditation

'There's nothing to worry about,' she told everyone who came to the house to ask how Lazarus was that day. 'He'll be well soon, because we've sent for Jesus. He'll be here any time now.'

'Mary, your brother is dying,' said the physician from Jerusalem. 'He can't possibly last through the night.'

She smiled confidently up into his grave face as she replied, 'But Jesus of Nazareth is a friend of ours. He loves Lazarus and me, and

---

*Listen! I stand at the door and knock; if anyone hears my voice and opens the door, I will come into his house and eat with him, and he will eat with me.* (Rev. 3:20, GNB)

our sister, Martha. If he heals strangers he's never even met before, and any old beggar who asks him, then he's absolutely sure to heal Lazarus – because he loves him. He'll be here in a minute, you'll see.'

However, by the next morning Lazarus was dead.

'No! You mustn't do that,' said Mary, as Martha began to pull the sheet up over the face they both loved so much. 'Don't you remember that story Peter is always telling us, about the young girl in Capernaum? She was dead at least an hour, but Jesus suddenly arrived, just in time, and brought her back to life. I'm going to the gate to look up the road for him. He'll be here soon.'

For hours she sat there, watching. 'Come on in, for goodness' sake!' snapped Martha. 'Can't you see how much you're leaving for me to do? We'll have half Jerusalem over here for the funeral. I've got hours of baking to do; come and give me a hand. Our brother will rise again at the resurrection on the last day. Mooning about out here won't bring him back any sooner.'

They buried Lazarus at sunset; and as they rolled the stone over the mouth of the grave, Mary's last hope was buried in the darkness with her brother.

Four days later, the funeral party was still going on, and Martha was far too busy to notice Mary. She sat motionless in the house, surrounded by crowds of friends and relations, but totally alone all the same. It was a comfort to know they were there, but she could not talk to them.

'She loved him so much,' they all said sadly, but how could she tell them the greatest agony was not the loss of Lazarus? Jesus hadn't come. He hadn't even sent a message to tell them why. She was exhausted from trying to understand him.

There was a commotion going on in the road outside, and children were shouting, 'He's coming down the road!'

'Quick, Mary,' said Martha, gripping her arm, 'Jesus is here – we must run to meet him before he reaches the village.'

Mary shook her head. Why should she go to him now? He hadn't come to her when she needed him. How could she possibly look him in the face, knowing he could so easily have prevented all this?

With a shrug of annoyance, Martha ran on without her and was met by this challenging question: 'I am the resurrection and the life, he that believes in me will live, even if he dies. Do you believe that?'

Her answer still echoes triumphantly down through the years. 'Yes, Lord, I believe you are the Christ . . .'

But Mary still sat motionless in the house. 'Come on, do!' protested Martha, shaking her crossly. 'He's asking for you!'

So she had no choice, she had to go. When she finally reached the place where he was waiting, all the emotions she had been holding down for so long finally burst out. 'If only you'd come, my brother wouldn't have died!' she exclaimed. She wanted to make him feel guilty – to pay him back for letting her down – yet she wanted so desperately to hold on to her dwindling faith in his love.

As Jesus watched, he could see the pain in her face as so many confusing emotions struggled beneath the surface. He did not ask her why she had not come out to meet him with Martha, why she had hidden away from him, looking for comfort from others instead of running to him. He did not compare her with Martha, whose faith was so strong. He did not reproach her for doubting him. He did not explain or answer her questions – he loved Mary too much to bother about any of those things. The only thing that mattered to him at that moment was the way she was feeling. As he stood there silently, he minded so much for her that he wept.

He loves you just as much as he loved Mary of Bethany. He is weeping for you too. Mary finally ran and flung herself at his feet. All he says to you at this moment is, 'Come to me.'

### A Prayer

*'Come to me, all of you who are tired from carrying heavy loads . . .'*
(Matt. 11:28, GNB)

Yes, Lord Jesus, I am tired; tired from carrying this load of grief and disappointment; tired of being reduced to a heap of bits and pieces; tired of struggling with all these conflicting feelings, and tired of making endless plans that I'm too tired to carry out. I can't possibly think about being built into anything new just yet – all I need is someone to comfort me because I'm hurting so badly. People I loved and things that I valued have been wrenched away, leaving my heart lacerated and bleeding. I feel as if I have been emotionally punched and beaten, and inside I'm nothing but bruises and festering wounds.

'*Come to me . . .*' (Matt. 11:28, GNB)

I think I can dare to come to you because you understand; you were beaten too. You were left wounded and humiliated to bear the pain of it all, alone.

'*Come to me . . . and I will give you rest.*' (Matt. 11:28, GNB)

Rest. Yes, I need rest so badly; but I'm restless with pain. Maybe rest means healing? If I exposed all these wounds to you, asked you to come into the pain with me, right to that hard core where it hurts most, would your love pour in to bathe the wounds, soothe the bruises and eventually bring perfect healing to my soul?

'*Come to me . . . "for I am the Lord, the one who heals you".*' (Exod. 15:26, GNB)

Lord Jesus, I do come to you and give you my bruises and sores, my conflict and confusion, and in exchange I receive your healing, comfort and rest for my weary soul.

---

*He jests at scars who never knew a wound.* (William Shakespeare)

## STOP FOR A MOMENT

'People say it was Jesus Christ who mended their broken lives, but how can a character from history help me now?'

*Jesus is not simply a character from history, though – he is actually God himself. He stepped down into our world and became a man, so he could show us what God is really like and how much he loves us.*

*He was constantly mending broken people. He healed bodies physically, but he cared about how people felt on the inside too.*

'What can a dead man do for me?'

*Jesus died a terrible death, but because he was God, death could not hold him. He rose after three days, and he still lives in this world today – still doing the same job of comforting, mending and restoring.*

'How is that possible?'

*The Bible tells us how the Spirit of Jesus returned forty days after his body had ascended to heaven. He no longer has a physical body, but he lives by his Spirit in the bodies of people who ask him to do so. When Jesus lives in a person by his Spirit, gradually he helps that person to think as he thinks, to see other people as he sees them, to feel about them as he feels about them, and to act towards them in the way he would act. The more room inside himself – or herself – that someone makes for Jesus, the more he is able to fill that person up with his personality and his power. That is what the word 'Christian' really means – someone who has Christ in their lives. Take out the letter 'a' in the word Christian and it spells 'Christ in'.*

I will lead my blind people by roads they have never travelled. I will turn their darkness into light . . . These are my promises and I will keep them. (Isa. 42:16, GNB)

# 3

# SHOCK AND DENIAL

Before we begin to examine in more detail the confusing kaleido-scope of reactions and emotions which usually follow any loss, perhaps we should look at the period when most of us feel nothing at all. Experts call this vacuum the stage of 'shock and denial'. This is how one of my friends described it:

'I was like a zombie, going through the motions of life quite automatically – without thinking about the past or the future. I just kept on doing silly little jobs to fill the time. People used to say, "Why don't you have a good cry, dear?" but I couldn't. I felt too discon-nected.'

Another friend said:

'I kept thinking, "This is only a bad dream, tomorrow I'll wake up and find everything's back to normal".'

## Shock

Perhaps this numbness is actually necessary. Our minds seem to need space to work through the implications of what has happened, so they switch off the emotions and render us incapable of feeling anything. In fact, shock seems to work for the mind rather like an anaesthetic works for a critically injured body, helping it over the worst part of the trauma.

Yet this anaesthetic effect can have its problems. We may lose the

> **But for you who revere my name, the sun of righteousness will rise with healing in its wings.** (Mal. 4:2, NIV)

bad feelings, but we can also lose the good feelings too, and, as I said in the last chapter, some people become very distressed because they feel they have 'gone dead' spiritually. When they find they have lost all the joy that prayer or worship once used to bring them, they fear they have lost God himself. This numb feeling can persist for months, so they think they are in the 'dark night of the soul', instead of in a normal stage of the grieving process.

On the other hand, shock can induce a feeling of euphoria. I remember lying in hospital in 1982 and being so relieved *not* to be dead that I felt marvellous – just as if I were floating in God's presence. All day, and most of the night, I listened to praise tapes on my personal stereo and was convinced life would always be like this. When I came home from hospital, I came down to earth with a nasty bump!

That bump seems to happen to a lot of other people, too. As the shock wears off, the full realisation of what has happened can be so painful that they retreat into the second part of the process: denial.

## Denial

When Granny went fishing about in that dustbin declaring indignantly, 'Anything can be mended,' she was denying the horrible possibility that her beautiful teapot might be permanently broken. The following people are all doing the same thing:

'He isn't going to be allowed to spoil my life; I'll find such a good solicitor that he'll be *made* to come back to me.'

'There *has* to be a doctor somewhere in the world who can make me well again.'

'My wife hasn't really got multiple sclerosis. The doctors must be wrong. It's all in her mind – she could walk if she tried.'

'Somewhere there must be someone who'll lend us enough money to get our business back on the road again.'

'Of course I'm not going deaf! The trouble is, young people nowadays can't be bothered to speak clearly.'

'God will heal me [or my child]. So many people are praying for us that he's bound to perform a miracle.'

> *God is light; in him there is no darkness at all.* (1 John 1:5, NIV)

### *Christians and denial*

I often used to think it would have been easier for me to 'adjust' to life as a disabled person if I did *not* believe in a God who answers prayer. I knew he had the power to put everything right for us, yet in spite of all the prayer that went up from our friends at church, he did not seem to be doing so!

Of course, humans must have hope or life is pointless; and when adversity strikes, it is right to fight back – and people with a tenacious will to survive recover much better than the pessimists who give up. However, there does come a time when it is right to face reality in order to adjust to things as they actually are. God wants to give us a new life, but he can't while we are still determined to reconstruct the old life. Jesus said, 'Happy are those who mourn; God will comfort them' (Matt. 5:4, GNB), but he cannot begin to comfort us until we admit we are broken and badly hurt.

### Beware of the 'Hold Up' Factor

The 'hold up' factor is what I consider the greatest danger we face during the whole mending process. All the stages we go through during this bizarre game of snakes and ladders are normal reactions, but it is vital to keep on moving through them. We must plod on continuously, taking each stage at a time and never allowing ourselves to stand still and become stuck in one particular attitude or thought pattern. For instance, it is normal to be angry when we are badly hurt, but if someone holds on to his or her anger for too long it becomes a way of life; such people then develop such huge chips on their shoulders that they seem to stay permanently trapped in the ruins of their 'broken teapot'.

There is a 'hold up' factor connected with each of the various stages that we will be considering in the next few chapters, and I will describe them all as we go along. People seem to get held up in this denial stage because they refuse to accept the event that has changed their lives. They do this in three ways:

> *The light that shines through the darkness – and the darkness can never extinguish it.* (John 1:5, LB)

1. They deny what has happened by insisting everything will be back to normal soon. The people I have just described, who refused to believe they would remain ill, alone or deaf, are examples of this.
2. They deny the pain of what has happened by not letting themselves feel their reactions.
3. They deny the event ever happened by 'forgetting' it completely – the 'buried video' approach (see p. 47).

## Everything Will Be Back to Normal

Perhaps the most extreme example of the first method mentioned that I have ever come across was when we were moving house. The estate agents sent us particulars of a very nice-sounding property in just the right area. We made an appointment and went round to see it. A woman of about forty-five opened the front door, and seemed quite happy to show us around her home. One of the bedrooms was obviously a child's room. School clothes were left out ready to wear on the bed, a cricket bat lay beside them, homework was spread out on the desk, and a model aeroplane was half finished on a table.

'How old's your son?' I asked, in order to make conversation.

'Eleven,' she replied proudly. 'He's a lovely boy.'

We liked the house very much, so we went to the agent and made an offer. Later that day, it was accepted. A week after that, our doorbell rang and the lady's husband stood on the step. He looked embarrassed, angry and distressed, in sequence, as he explained that the sale was off.

'It's happened so many times before. I nearly get her to the point of moving, but in the end she can never face it. You see, our only son was killed eight years ago. She just can't bring herself to believe he has really gone. She feels she has to wait there for him with everything ready in case he comes home one day. But life has to go on, doesn't it?' he finished, and there was a note of desperation in his voice.

> *Once the little child in us is healed, then the adult can get on with their life.* (Russ Parker)

### Denying the Pain

This is the second way that people get held up in the denial stage, and I met someone like that when I was asked to speak at a Ladies' Day held in a church in the North of England. The 'hub' of the proceedings was a lady called Rose, who won my complete admiration by her ability to dispense tea for a hundred thirsty women at frequent intervals, cracking a continuous string of jokes while she did so.

'Isn't she wonderful?' whispered someone in my left ear. 'Her son committed suicide a few months back. He got very depressed after he failed his exams, but she never talks about it.'

As I was speaking that day, I kept on seeing Rose's face as she listened through the kitchen hatch. Her expression was frozen and quite without emotion. At the end of the day, when most people had left, I was just putting on my coat when she hurried up to me. 'Thought you might like a quick cuppa before you go,' she said, holding out yet another paper mug.

'You look tired,' I said, 'after all that tea pouring.'

'I'm all right,' she replied firmly, 'but I think I may have something wrong with my throat. It feels so tight and painful these days, I can't seem to swallow.'

'Could I pray about that?' I asked her gently. She nodded, and we closed our eyes as we stood there side by side in the empty hall. As soon as I began to pray I had a vivid picture. The whole of Rose's throat and chest was filled with a huge block of ice. I described it to her and then I said, 'Rose, I think it's made of all the tears you can't seem to shed. They're frozen solid, and they'll do a lot of damage if you don't allow Jesus to melt them with the warmth of his love.'

'I can't cry,' she replied firmly. 'It wouldn't be a good witness if I gave in to it. And there's no point in getting all emotional, you've just got to put on a brave face and get on with it, haven't you?'

---

*Something in us prevents us from remembering, when remembering proves to be too difficult or painful . . . We are not entirely successful however, because the memory is buried within us, and influences every moment of our growth. Sometimes it breaks through the prison and strikes at us directly and painfully.* (Paul Tillich)

'Rose,' I said, 'just because you are a Christian does not mean you are exempt from pain.' I got her to sit down, and even managed to make her drink my tea while I talked. 'When Jesus was a baby, Mary and Joseph met an old man one day called Simeon. He knew exactly who this tiny baby really was, and he was so delighted that he took him in his arms and thanked God. Then suddenly he looked up into Mary's face and the smile died away from his eyes. She must have looked so happy that day, but Simeon was "seeing" her thirty-three years later, bent with grief as she stood by the cross where her son was dying in agony. "A sword will pierce your own soul too" (Luke 2:35, NIV), he murmured quietly. Rose, a terrible thing has happened to you. It must feel exactly as if a "sword has pierced your soul". You are wounded just as severely as if you had been stabbed physically. If you ignored a stab wound, you'd bleed seriously and probably go into shock. Or the wound might become infected and cause all kinds of severe problems. I think you badly need to ask Jesus to treat this wound of yours.'

'No!' she said, as her clenched fist squashed the empty paper cup to pulp. 'If I start to cry, I'll never stop.' And with that, she hurried away towards the kitchen.

'Isn't she wonderful!' The same woman was talking again into my left ear. Like so many other Christians, Rose simply did not realise how dangerous it can be to freeze her feelings.

### Why do we get stuck like this?

I am beginning to wonder if sometimes we get stuck because we are unwilling to face the issue of who we really blame for what happened. For instance, there is Beth, who was disabled after her car skidded on a patch of ice. Beth admitted she had not been concentrating too well that morning, but the accident seemed to be 'just one of those things'. Five years later, Beth finally managed to admit that deep down she had always felt her lack of concentration was due to sleepless nights spent worrying over her rebellious teenage daughter. Secretly, she had felt so bitter that their relationship had broken down completely.

---

*Freedom is what we have – Christ has set us free!* (Gal. 5:1, GNB)

---

'But surely it's not very nice to go looking for scapegoats to blame for all our troubles?' people say. 'And it doesn't matter, anyway.' But it *does* matter, because our subconscious minds know exactly who we are blaming for all our misfortunes. While our 'culprits' lurk down there like nameless shadows, shaped like a question mark, they can hold us back from the new life ahead because no one can 'let go' of a shadow.

Discovering that I had been blaming God for allowing me to be ill, and being able to leave behind those grudges in the cow dung, was the moment my 'teapot' began to mend. Rose, denying the pain she felt after her son's death, did become quite ill soon after we met. It was nothing serious, just infections that would not clear up and exhaustion that her doctor put down to depression. In the end, she had to give up her job and church work for a while.

Looking back now, she realises she dared not allow all that grief to be released because there was so much anger tangled up amongst it. She could not bring herself to admit it, but subconsciously she was furious with her son for committing suicide. She was also angry that he had allowed himself to drift into the unsavoury relationships and destructive activities that she felt had led to his depression and death.

One day, when she was visiting her doctor, she exploded – and finally managed to put into words all the resentment she had been hiding for over a year. 'How could he do such a thing to us?' she asked the doctor, and then felt terrible as soon as the words were out.

'The doctor was so kind,' she told me later. 'He said a lot of people feel angry like that after someone dies, even as a result of an accident, but he said I would have to let my son go before I could move on through my journey of grieving. He was right, too. That was the day I managed to cry – in fact, my husband thought I was never going to stop. Somehow everything came to the surface, and finally I did manage to get rid of it all. It was a turning point for me, and things have been much better since then.'

---

**You will know the truth, and the truth shall set you free.**
(John 8:32, GNB)

### The 'Buried Video'

Some people not only deny their feelings, but they wipe the event that caused those feelings right out of their memories. The usual way for our minds to cope with traumatic events is by 'reliving' them endlessly for a while. The memories of all we have seen and felt go round and round in our heads like an endless video replay. Although it can be most distressing, this internal video is part of the mind's natural healing mechanism, and after a while the repetitive memory fades or the replays become less frequent. Sometimes, however, the experience is too painful to handle, so we simply 'bury the video'. In other words, we exclude all the bad memories from our minds. For a short period of time this might work quite well as a coping strategy, so long as we are willing to recall the incident and work through our reactions to it as soon as we feel strong enough. The problems begin when we continuously refuse to dig that video up again. The human mind never forgets anything, so the original incident remains in the subconscious like a festering wound, causing irrational fears, behaviour problems or difficult relationships.

I know all this is true because long ago when I was a child I 'buried a video' that has caused me trouble for the last forty years. It is only recently that I finally managed to dig it up and dared to watch it again. Perhaps if I explain how I was helped to do this, it might encourage other people whose 'teapots' broke when they were children.

### The 'Teapot' that Broke Long Ago

In June 1991 Tony and I went together to a Communion Service in a church that we do not usually attend. That morning, the Gospel reading was from Matthew 6:14–15, and for some reason these words seemed to stick in my mind: 'For if you forgive men when they sin against you, your heavenly Father will also forgive you. But if you do not forgive men their sins, your Father will not forgive your sins.'

'Goodness!' I thought, 'those are strong words.' I have a terrible

---

*If the Son sets you free, then you will be really free.* (John 8:36, GNB)

habit of daydreaming in church, and suddenly I 'saw' myself arriving eagerly at the gates of heaven, only to be told by St Peter, 'Sorry, luvvy, there was that person you said you couldn't forgive, but really you meant you *wouldn't* forgive. So you can't come in here because your own sins aren't forgiven.'

The idea was so nasty that I shuddered and returned to earth rather rapidly. 'But do I have anyone I need to forgive?' I asked myself. I couldn't think of anyone at all, so I tried to concentrate on the sermon that had just begun.

This was on forgiveness, too, and the preacher talked about the man Jesus described in Matthew 5 who came to worship God at the altar carrying his offering. Jesus pointed out that it was useless for him to try to worship God because he was holding a grudge against his brother. He had to put down his offering and go at once to try to put right that broken relationship.

'The matter was so urgent, he even had to do it before the closing hymn!' declared the preacher, glaring at us severely from the pulpit. Perhaps he had the same naughty imagination as I have, but he made his point so well that several people wriggled uncomfortably. 'So don't come up to take communion this morning until you are *sure* you are willing to lay down anything you hold against someone else,' he concluded, and I felt relieved I had no grudges on my conscience. All the same, I felt I had better make quite sure, so I said the quick prayer that was to have a monumental effect on my life.

'Lord, please show me if there *is* someone I need to forgive.' It was when we reached the Lord's Prayer that the familiar words I must have said a thousand times suddenly stuck in my throat. 'Forgive us our sins as we forgive those who sin against us . . .'

In my head I heard a harsh voice shouting, 'Jennifer Rees, you are the stupidest child I have ever had the misfortune to teach!' I smiled – almost fondly. 'That was Miss Mitchell,' I thought. 'Surely God can't be serious, I'm not upset about that poor old thing – I can hardly remember her, and anyway she was quite right to call me stupid!'

At seven I had been sent to a private school for girls, and I soon discovered I was the only one in the class who couldn't read. (I was fourteen before I finally mastered the art.) When I tried to write down

---

*I feel I'm on a journey and I don't know where I'm headed, but I trust the driver.* (Roy Castle)

all the stories that teamed in my brain, no one could read the jumble of back-to-front words and bizarre spelling. Maths was no better because I could never work out whether five was more or less than seven, and I caused chaos in gym lessons because I did not know my left from my right, and always marched in a different direction to everyone else! Nowadays, all those problems would have been given some fancy name, but words such as 'dyslexia' were not invented when I was at school, so they labelled me 'backward' instead. Poor Miss Mitchell was lumbered with me in her class for four years – everyone else moved up in September, but not me.

By the time I was eleven I was so totally humiliated that I ran away and refused to go back to any school – ever again. They call that by another name these days, 'school phobia', but it felt to me like cowardice - and I have been deeply ashamed of it ever since.

In church that day I couldn't really think of anything I needed to forgive Miss Mitchell *for*, but just to make sure I said a hasty 'I forgive her Lord', before going up to the communion rail. Yet I had no idea as I knelt there just how many memories and feelings I was pushing down behind my tranquil expression. I had become so used to smothering them, I did not even realise I was doing so.

### The recurring nightmare

The first thing I noticed after that service was that my recurring nightmare happened more frequently than usual. Ever since I ran away from school I constantly dreamed I was being dragged back to face a sea of jeering faces and swirling navy gym slips. I had never taken much notice because frequent dreaming is an occupational hazard for most writers, and anyway it was so lovely waking up to find I was an adult safely in bed beside my husband.

Then two months later I had a letter. It was from the only girl who had been my friend in those four years at school. We had never met, or even been in touch, since the day I ran away.

'Let's make a date and get together,' said her letter. I looked

For the Sprit that God has given us does not make us timid; instead, his Spirit fills us with power, love, and self-control. (2 Tim. 1:7, GNB)

forward to seeing her again, but was rather disappointed to find she no longer had pigtails and a brace on her teeth!

'At least you're a bit slimmer than you used to be,' she said.

'Yes, I was as fat as a barrel, wasn't I!' I laughed. At least I could remember that, but reminiscing about old times was surprisingly difficult for me, because I seemed to have 'lost' those years almost entirely.

'Miss Mitchell was a marvellous games teacher,' said my friend nostalgically, 'but I don't think she liked you very much!'

'I can't really remember her,' I said vaguely as I tried not to hear that voice shouting across the netball pitch: 'You're supposed to *catch* the ball, not stand there until it hits you! You're too revoltingly fat to walk, let alone run!'

'I've got a photo of her,' my friend said, as she rummaged in her bag. 'I took it last year at the school's centenary.' I went ice cold all over as I looked down at the face I had 'forgotten', and found that in reality I remembered it in minute detail. It seemed quite extraordinary that a woman of fifty could be so terrified of a mere photograph, but I was so afraid that I felt sick. I was oddly angry too. 'How dare she say I was stupid!' I thought, 'And how could she make the whole class laugh and jeer at me?' Hastily, I pushed these awkward emotions back in the dark cellar where I had been hiding them for forty years, and I managed to pin the smile firmly back on my face as I handed back the photo. 'Good job I've forgiven Miss Mitchell,' I thought, as I locked the cellar door once again.

But I had not really forgiven her at all, because I would not allow myself to acknowledge how much she had hurt me. It is foolish to say, 'Forgive and forget,' because we can't forgive until we are willing to *remember*, and that was something I was far too afraid to do just then. Until we identify the person who damaged us, we will never be free of the damage that person caused.

> *For God . . . made his light shine in our hearts to give us the light of the knowledge of the glory of God in the face of Christ.* (2 Cor. 4:6, NIV)

### Getting to the root

About eighteen months later, something happened that at the time I did not realise was connected with Miss Mitchell. I went to see my great friend Marilyn Baker, the blind singer, and her companion, Tracy, who is deaf. I respect their ministry of inner healing greatly. Marilyn can 'see' things and Tracy can 'hear' things that most people with ordinary sight and hearing never perceive at all.

I went to them because of a very long-standing problem of my own. Perhaps we all have a besetting sin, something that seems to grow up in our lives like a tangling weed, getting in the way of the good things and spoiling them. We keep cutting it down, but it shoots up again to defeat us. I had been grappling with my very embarrassing 'weed' for years, and was totally sick of it. 'I need to get at the root of this thing,' I kept thinking, 'then perhaps it could be pulled out once and for all.' So just after Christmas I went all the way round the M25 to Watford, hoping that Marilyn and Tracy might 'hear' and 'see' what the Lord wanted to say to me.

My 'weed' was an eating problem. I was a fat child, I became an even fatter teenager, and then in my early twenties I developed anorexia to the point where I resembled a skeleton. Ever since then I have struggled with the humiliating misery of compulsive eating followed by endless starvation diets. I told Marilyn and Tracy all about it, and added, 'I've put on so much weight recently I don't have anything in my wardrobe I can wear!'

They listened to the Lord silently for a time, then Tracy said, 'I feel the root of all this has something to do with words that were spoken to you once. Perhaps by a teacher?' I felt startled because I certainly had never mentioned Miss Mitchell. Then Tracy added, 'Her words have also caused you to drive yourself because of a vow you made.'

I could see that being told so often I was stupid could have accounted for the crushing sense of inadequacy and failure that has dogged me for forty years. I have always driven myself to ridiculous limits to prove I am not as inadequate as I fear I am. So I guessed I must once have vowed to prove Miss Mitchell wrong, but how could she possibly be responsible for making me fat?

---

*In him was life and that life was the light of men.* (John 1:4, NIV)

So Marilyn and Tracy prayed a prayer to cut me off from the vow I could not remember making, and I drove home – eating several bars of chocolate on the way and feeling that I had failed yet again! Now, though, I believe that their prayers made possible what happened a month later.

It was late in January when I went to the North of England to give a talk entitled 'The Power of Words'. I explained how the things people say to us can bind us almost like a curse, changing the very way we think and feel about ourselves. By way of illustration, I mentioned Miss Mitchell and how her words had made me feel I was always a worthless failure. I also said I had 'forgiven' her, and that I believed the way to be freed from the effects of harmful words was to forgive the person who originally spoke them to us.

It all sounded quite good and everyone seemed to be nodding in agreement, but I was in for a nasty shock! In the meeting that night was a missionary teacher called Ann. She and I had been pen friends for years, so we arranged to meet for coffee before I returned home the following day.

'There is something I feel I must say,' she began awkwardly. 'You haven't forgiven Miss Mitchell at all, have you?' I was stunned.

'Yes I have,' I protested.

'Something tells me you have only forgiven her in your mind,' said Ann, 'but not from the heart – because in your heart you hate her.'

'I've never hated anyone in my life,' I protested. 'I think I was terribly frightened of her, but . . .'

'Have you seen her lately?'

'Oh no,' I said hastily, 'I never want to see her again.'

'That's the problem then,' replied Ann. 'You're only in the first stage of forgiving – the part that happens inside us – but the second part is all about moving towards the other person to offer forgiveness in a tangible way. When we have been hurt we shrink away from the person who inflicted the pain by "keeping out of their way", but while we are still doing that we are only at the half-way mark. I think you should go to that teacher of yours.'

'I really can't see the point,' I said, 'and anyway I used to think she was *ancient* forty years ago. If she's still alive, she must be about a

---

*True grieving uncovers the wounds and mourns them with painful energy until healing is achieved.* (Mary Pytches)

hundred and fifty by now.' But I knew Ann was looking at me with her kind, but penetrating, brown eyes. 'All right,' I said at last, 'when I get home I'll see if I can trace her.'

The secretary of my old school was most helpful when I rang. Miss Mitchell was alive and well, she told me, and even gave me a phone number. I was shaking all over as I tried to make my thanks sound sincere. Even after a strong cup of tea, I still could not muster up enough courage to ring the number on my notepad, so I took my dog Brodie for a walk in the park and tried to think what I could say when I finally managed to dial it.

In the park, my speech sounded very mature, confident and business-like, but once I heard that familiar voice say, 'Yes? Speak up, can't you?' I was reduced to a quivering child who was almost too afraid to remember her own name. I realised she had always been able to make me feel like that, and the louder she had shouted at me, the more stupid I became.

'I was in your form,' I managed at last, 'for four years. I wondered if I could just pop in s-some t-time, there's s-something I want to give you.' Well, there was! I wanted to give her my forgiveness, even if I intended to express it through a bunch of flowers rather than in words.

'How about next Tuesday at eleven – sharp?' suggested Miss Mitchell. I thanked her profusely and collapsed in a sweaty heap in my armchair. I was not at all sure I could go through with this, and my feelings towards Ann at that moment were far from affectionate.

An awful lot seemed to happen inside me during that week. Tony was away on a conference in the Ukraine, so I had plenty of time to watch the 'videos' I had buried for so long. I began to realise just how many of my lifelong problems could be traced back to those four years in my childhood. The more I thought about the things that had crushed and broken something inside me, the less I wanted to go near the person I felt was responsible. And what was I going to say to her? That question worried me considerably. 'All is forgiven' sounded perfectly ridiculous! And had I really forgiven her anyway?

The whole situation seemed too much for me to handle, until one

---

*The deaf and dumb sign language for forgiveness is signed by wiping the palm of one hand firmly across the other as if removing any stain or mess that clings to it.* (Russ Parker)

morning when I was reading Luke 6 in an amplified version of the New Testament, and I realised Jesus told us to 'Pray for the happiness of those who curse you, implore God's favour upon those who abuse you – who revile, reproach, disparage and high-handedly misuse you' (6:28, AMP). I was beginning to blame Miss Mitchell for doing all those things to me, but Jesus knew what he was about when he told us to pray for our own particular enemy because, as I soon discovered, prayer has the most remarkable effect.

First of all, it kills hate. As I prayed for Miss Mitchell, I pictured myself bringing her into the presence of God, and the two of us standing side by side before him. Somehow it is impossible to stand there like that with ice-cold anger in your heart. God's love seems to melt it away like snow in the morning sun.

Prayer also began to help me see her from God's angle instead of my own. As I prayed, I began to wonder if some hurt that Miss Mitchell had once received could have caused her to be so aggressive. Then about three days later, I discovered the answer to that question. Someone who had known Miss Mitchell for many years was able to tell me about the terrible things that had happened to her as a child. There is an old French proverb that says, 'To understand all is to forgive all.' I was not sure I was quite ready to 'forgive all', but it certainly helped me to understand.

Then one morning, as I was asking the Lord yet again how to handle my Tuesday visit, I suddenly realised I was not going to Miss Mitchell to offer some grand gesture of forgiveness: the main purpose of my visit was to ask *her* to forgive *me*! It is a terrible thing to hate someone for so many years and to blame them for all your personal weaknesses and failures. As I looked up everything Jesus said about forgiving, and searched the commentaries in order to understand what he meant, I began to realise that forgiving means 'setting free'. The Greek word is *aphesis*, the same word Jesus uses at the grave of Lazarus when he emerged all bound up like an Egyptian mummy. By not forgiving Miss Mitchell, perhaps I could have bound her spiritually by the grudges I held against her. Some commentators think that this is what Jesus meant when he said, 'Whatever you bind on earth will be bound in heaven, and whatever you loose on earth will be loosed in heaven' (Matt. 18:18, NIV).

There was another verse I discovered that week: 'If you forgive anyone's sins, they are forgiven. If you refuse to forgive them, they are unforgiven' (John 20:23, LB). Did that mean that as I prayed for Miss Mitchell I was saying to God, 'Please let her off the eternal punishment I feel she deserves for hurting me'? Could this be what Jesus meant when he told us to show mercy (Luke 6:36)? It was all getting a bit too deep for someone like me. However, I was not so stupid that I could not understand that I had sinned by hating her for so long and blaming her for so much. I felt I had to confess that to God as quickly as possible.

Then the horrendous thought struck me. Would I have to *ask* for her forgiveness too? The idea sent me into a panic. It was bad enough to imagine facing someone who completely terrified me and saying, 'I forgive you,' without having to tell her about the resentment I had felt towards her as well. Of course, I knew that would not be what God wanted me to do in a literal sense. It would feel more like a spiteful revenge than an act of penitence to let her know she had been hated for so long. No, it would be the attitude of heart in which I went that mattered, and I prayed that if it was possible to express the sentiment in some way that did not cause her pain, that God would show me how to do it. In the event, that is exactly what he did.

### The willingness to forgive

By the Monday, so many thoughts were churning and tumbling about inside me that I must have been very hard to live with, and the three 'overgrown' children who are still at home had a very rough time.

'You must be going senile, Mum!' said Duncan, and even Brodie looked offended. During the evening, I decided to look out a photo of myself as a child to take with me the following day – so at least Miss Mitchell might have some chance of remembering me. I went rummaging through the box from the attic until I found one that must have been taken very soon after my first day at the school. I sat holding it for a long time, looking at the small, thin face that stared apprehensively up at me. 'That child looks haunted,' I thought, and when I went to bed I put the photo on the table beside me.

I never sleep well when Tony is away, and the thought of that

---

General James Oglethorpe said to John Wesley, 'I'll never forgive!' John Wesley replied, 'Then I hope, Sir, that you will never sin.' (John Wesley, quoted by David Augsburger)

appointment the next morning certainly did not help matters. At about two o'clock I finally gave up trying to sleep and put the light on. Often when I wake like that it seems to be because the Lord wants me to pray in a specific way, so I asked him if that was the case now.

Suddenly I thought, 'but the child in the photo is *thin*!' My mental impression of myself as a child was that I was always grotesquely fat, rather like a Miss Piggy puppet, but the child in the photo could have been accurately described as 'skinny'. Therefore I must have got fat after my first day at school.

### Reliving the event

As I sat up in bed looking at the photo, something began to happen that I think was one of the most extraordinary experiences of my life. If I had not described it on paper the next day, I would not believe it really happened. The memories that I had buried became so vivid that I felt I really was back at school again. I could smell the distinctive 'cloakroom' aroma, which was a blend of stale sweat, disinfectant and old plimsoles – with a dash of cooked cabbage from the kitchens close by. I felt that sick feeling of desolation that always came when my mother dropped me off at the door, and then drove home without me. Quite abandoned, I was left to face probable annihilation all alone. I could see the child in the photo as if she was nothing to do with me, although I seemed to know how she was feeling.

In my hand I was clutching a grimy arithmetic book full of the sums I had got wrong the day before – all eighty of them. I had been told to take them home and get them right overnight – or else. I had worked at them until I was too tired to think straight, refusing all offers of help, because I felt Miss Mitchell would know, and that would make it even worse – for she loathed cheats.

Why don't children tell their parents when they are being bullied or abused? It took me four years until I dared to explain what school was really like. Whyever did I wait so long? Perhaps because I felt too ashamed, and this is probably true for others as well. I believed Miss Mitchell when she said I was the stupidest child she knew, and I remember the way my mother had looked when she was told I was backward. Both my parents were brilliantly gifted and extremely attractive people, and I always felt that I was a great embarrassment to them – particularly when I grew so enormously fat. So I never 'told' because I felt it was all my fault they had a dud for a daughter.

So there I stood, cringing with fright, clutching a book full of sums that were bound to be wrong and facing yet another day of insults, derision and humiliation – perhaps even physical pain. I could feel the rumble of hundreds of feet pounding the boarded corridor and suddenly I was right in my own nightmare, as girls in gym slips swarmed around me shouting contemptuously, 'You're a fat moron – a thick idiot!' Then I could hear her shouting. She was coming towards me through the crowd – nearer and nearer – and I felt sick with an old familiar dread.

'Lord!' I muttered, 'Help me!'

### Warning!

It is never right, or safe, to relive painful memories alone. We must go back to the place where we were hurt with Jesus himself beside us, and preferably some other friend as well.

None of mine were handy at two o'clock in the morning, but my urgent cry for help was answered instantly. I sensed Jesus really was there. I seemed to see him standing beside that small, thin, frightened child, with one big, kind hand on her shoulder. As the face of the monster loomed closer, distorted with rage, the hand on the child's shoulders tightened reassuringly, then just as the monster was ready to strike he stepped between her and me, taking the abuse, the pain and the misery himself – because he cared so much. In my head I heard these words ringing like church bells on Christmas morning: 'Surely he has borne our griefs and carried our sorrows, (Isa. 53:4, AV). 'The insults which are hurled at you have fallen on me' (Rom. 15:3, GNB).

Suddenly, it was all over. The child was free for ever from the memory, because *he* had borne everything in my place. I sensed there was something very important that I needed to do after that, and I realised the child in the photo was saying, 'Miss Mitchell, I forgive you freely for everything you did or said to me. I let go of all blame and set you free from the grudges I have carried against you ever since. And please forgive me for hating you and binding you so long.'

It had been no use forgiving Miss Mitchell as an adult on behalf of the child I had once been. One adult can easily forgive another, because as adults we also have power, and we forget just how small and helpless a child can feel. We need to relive by memory the painful events to make real forgiving possible. Exactly the same applies to forgiving any hurt, even if it happened last week. We must not deny the pain we felt, and we need to go back mentally to the moment our 'enemy' hurt us so that we can release forgiveness to them at the point in our memory when the damage was done.

### Healing the wounds

Suddenly Miss Mitchell was gone, as was the school – and the cloakroom smell – but I was aware that the child was still hurt and in need of healing. She had been emotionally wounded so many times in those four years. 'Watching our buried videos' helps us understand these wounds, but only Jesus himself can heal them and set us free from their destructive effects. So I asked him to do that, and later during that long night something very strange happened. I 'saw' another picture. Jesus himself was sitting at the foot of a huge wooden cross holding the child that had once been me. At first I was pleased, until I realised she was wriggling about, restless and fretful. 'Lord, whyever isn't that child more contented?' I asked indignantly.

His reply was perfectly clear and plain, 'She will not allow me to comfort her and she grows into an adult who will not always turn to me for comfort, either.' He looked so sad that I really felt mortified, and I sat there for a long time trying to think what he could mean. Then another memory came back into my mind. I saw myself walking into the sweetshop on my way home from school. My mother, who was generous to a fault, always heaped me with pocket money and I would go in and buy quantities of chocolate and toffees each day.

Somehow the sweets eased the pain of the day and made life seem bearable again. I would still eat a huge tea when I arrived home, and go on nicking and picking all evening. No one ever seemed to notice. It was no wonder I was soon too fat to play netball! Obviously it was not a sin at the time, for the child in me had been crying out for love and acceptance. It was then, though, that I discovered a method of easing pain that I have used countless times ever since, instead of going direct to the Lord for comfort. I had deliberately turned away from him and craved the counterfeit comfort of food.

So here was the root of my lifelong 'weed', and I asked the Lord to pull it out, once and for all. I believe that he did. I had asked him thousands of times before, but perhaps I could not be forgiven and delivered until that night when I finally forgave the person I subconsciously blamed for causing it all. Surely it is as we forgive that we can be forgiven.

Then the word 'fear' kept coming into my mind, and I realised that fear had also become one of my 'weeds', causing everything from chronic worry to a total inability to face certain situations. If I ever encounter someone aggressive and angry, I simply go to pieces – and all those endless feelings of inadequacy stem from the same root. Of course, fear itself is not a sin, but running away from it can be. And some of the more subtle techniques I have devised to avoid the things I fear have been very wrong indeed.

It is also not a sin to feel inadequate, but it *is* wrong to drive yourself unmercifully to prove that you are not. Misplaced energy like that can destroy relationships, and it must be a terrible strain living with someone who constantly has to prove she is 'Super-woman' – in case the world realises just how stupid she actually is!

Suddenly I remembered the day I made the vow Tracy had mentioned. I had been standing in the middle of a field full of stubble one autumn, when I was about ten. I remembered the flocks of migrating birds swirling in the sky above my head as I said, 'In spite of what I am, somehow I'll make my parents proud of me one day.' As well as removing the seed of fear that night, I believe the Lord delivered me from the bondage of achievement hunting and the slavery to other people's desires and expectations.

It was about five-thirty in the morning when I finally knew it was all done. I felt as if I'd had a major operation – as indeed I had – but I also felt gloriously free. Just as I was falling asleep I saw the figure of Jesus walking away into the distance with a little girl holding his hand. She hopped and danced away with him in the kind of carefree abandonment she would never have known forty years before.

### We are not stuck for ever with the damage

Sometimes when people 'watch their childhood videos', they can think, 'I'm stuck with all these problems because of what was done to me!' But after all that happened to me that night, I really do believe that inner healing and deliverance from the tangling weeds of sin come through being willing to allow Jesus to help us forgive the people who hurt us. It dawned on me that night just how ridiculous I was to hold someone from my childhood responsible for causing all my weaknesses and failures.

It is not what people do to us that cripples us, but how we react to what they do. I chose to allow the roots of those weeds of sin to remain and grow in me through the years. I was not responsible for what people did to me, or did not do, but I *was* responsible for how I coped with it – for the food, the desire to prove them all wrong, and the fear that makes me run away.

## The second part of forgiving

As I drove up the hill towards Miss Mitchell's cottage the following morning I have to admit I was so terrified that I had to grip the steering wheel very tightly indeed. I knew that the 'child me' had been set free the night before, but the 'adult me' felt a perfect fool! I still didn't know what I was going to say and the flowers on the back seat had cost far more than I could afford. In fact, as the car turned into her drive I couldn't help thinking that the first half of forgiving, the bit that happens in our own hearts, is an awful lot easier than the second part – when we have to do something that demonstrates it!

By one minute past eleven, I was sitting nervously on the very edge of my chair in Miss Mitchell's front room. I was very much the little girl and I could hear myself prattling and giggling like an eight-year-old. 'For goodness' sake, get a grip on yourself!' I told myself furiously. 'Remember you've published sixteen books, so you can't be completely inadequate!'

She must have realised I had something on my mind, and she came to my rescue by cutting abruptly across the chatter.

'Why did you come?'

'To lay some ghosts,' I said nervously. 'I wasn't very happy at school, you see.' She looked surprised. 'I couldn't read, if you remember, or write, either.' Then I took a deep breath and added something I had wanted to say to her so many times during the years in between. 'Nowadays, they would say I was dyslexic.'

She looked at me so strangely I wasn't quite sure what she was thinking. Then at last she said, 'Yes, we didn't know much about that kind of thing in my day. We used to tell parents of difficult children that their offspring were either lazy or thick.' I cringed, but then she added, 'I think perhaps we might have been rather cruel.' I am not sure if she meant it as a kind of indirect apology, but I certainly took it as such.

After that, conversation became much easier and we both relaxed. When she finally showed me out, something very significant happened. She said, 'I'm sorry you were unhappy at school.' I reached out and took the hand I had been so afraid of as a child, and held it for a moment. 'Well I'm sure that wasn't your fault,' I replied. 'You couldn't have known how I felt, could you?' And we kissed each other warmly.

The transaction was done, we had both offered and received forgiveness, and we parted with promises to meet again. As I drove home, I felt a great sense of peace.

I was fortunate to have such a gracious 'enemy', but reconciliations are not always made so easily. You will find some practical tips from other people in the chapter on forgiveness (Chapter 11). There are also some ideas for expressing forgiveness to someone who has died.

---

## A Meditation

It was one of those awkward step-families, where everyone has the same father, but different mothers – so no one knows quite where they belong. He was almost the youngest of twelve, and that did not help him either, but the fact that his father adored him caused his greatest problem. His older brothers hated him for it. Of course, he never imagined their jealousy would drive them to such terrible lengths, so he was taken totally by surprise when one day on a lonely hillside they grabbed him and threw him down the shaft of an old, dry well. He had seen murder glinting in their eyes, so as he huddled in the darkness waiting for them to come back, he was convinced they would pull him out and slit his throat. In the end it was greed that saved his life. His brothers found a way of making some money, as well as ridding themselves of him for ever.

Perhaps in the hard, lonely years of slavery that lay ahead, or during his imprisonment in the dungeons of Egypt, Joseph may often have wished he had died quickly at their hands instead of having to face all the suffering his brothers caused him. Did he block out the memories of his childhood? Perhaps he did, because when life improved for him and he even became Prime Minister, he did not go straight back to find the father who had loved him so much, nor did he even send him a reassuring message.

Then one day, there they were, standing before him in the state reception room of his grand home: the ten brothers who had mocked him as a child, robbed him of the best years of his life, and hated him so much they had tried to destroy him. So many memories must have come flooding back into his mind, but he could not tell them who he was because he couldn't forgive – not then – because it all still hurt too much.

For months or even years he struggled with his emotions. One moment he was weeping like a child at the joy of seeing them again, the next he was harshly throwing them into gaol. He lavished good things on them and then played cruel tricks, hiding money in their grain sacks, seizing one as a hostage, and accusing another of stealing his silver cup. Then when he had finally proved to himself that their hearts were no longer as black as he had always feared they were, he called them in and forgave them. It felt as if the wall of a dam had finally given way as all the pent-up pain and grief finally gushed out, and he cried so loudly that everyone in the palace could hear him.

However, many years later, the writer of Genesis tells us that Joseph's brothers were still not quite sure they were truly forgiven:

> When Joseph's brothers saw that their father was dead, they said, 'What if Joseph holds a grudge against us and pays us back for all the wrongs we did to him?' . . . His brothers then came and threw themselves down before him. 'We are your slaves,' they said. But Joseph said to them, 'Don't be afraid. Am I in the place of God? You intended to harm me, but God intended it for good to accomplish what is now being done, the saving of many lives. So then, don't be afraid. I will provide for you and your children.' And he reassured them and spoke kindly to them. (Gen. 50:15–21, NIV)

## A Prayer

### *For those who find it hard to face life as it is*

'*Come to me all you who are tired from fighting reality . . . "for the Spirit that God has given us does not make us timid; instead, his Spirit fills us with power, love, and self-control"*.' (2 Tim. 1:7, GNB)

Lord Jesus, I am afraid – I don't want it all to be like this. I can't bear to live through one more day feeling like this. Yet I know you understand how I feel. You did not want your life to go the way it did either. You wanted people to listen to what you had come to tell them, not turn against you and reject the love you offered them. You did not want to go up to Jerusalem and face the final horror. Yet you set your face like flint – and went. You looked hard at reality, and had the courage to move towards it. Help me not to shrink away. Help me to set my face towards reality as you set yours. I give you this feeling of dread and foreboding, and in its place I receive your courage.

### For those who find it hard to face life as it was

'*Come to me all you who are tired of fighting the dark shadows of the past* . . . *"for I am the light of the world. Whoever follows me will* . . . *have the light of life".*' (John 8:12, NIV)

Lord Jesus, come with me into the darkness of the cellar where I have hidden so many frightening things. I've shoved feelings down there because there wasn't time to process them – memories I couldn't face, emotions I thought were wrong and must be suppressed, fears, doubts, resentment, and yes, furious anger! Shine your light on these things I never wanted to see again, and help me remember things I would much rather forget. Handle my reactions with me, and show me how to bear the pain of it all. I am so afraid of the dark; please come with me, and one by one we can bring these things to the surface and out into your sunlight. Lord, I am ashamed that I felt as I did, and as I still do. Forgive me, heal me, help me to let it go. I give you my darkness, and in exchange I receive your light.

## Perhaps the Lord Would Respond Like This

'The people walking in darkness have seen a great light; on those living in the land of the shadow of death a light has dawned.' (Isa. 9:2, NIV)
'Arise, shine, for your light has come, and the glory of the Lord rises upon you.' (Isa. 60:1, NIV)

## STOP FOR A MOMENT

*Refusing to forgive and harbouring anger damages our bodies, our minds and our spirits.*

### Physical Damage

*Modern research is leading many doctors to believe there is a definite link between negative emotion and some types of physical illness. Work done by doctors such as Friedman and Simonton conclude that unresolved anger and guilt can trigger and maintain some forms of heart disease and certain types of cancer. Other researchers feel that the same link exists in some rheumatic conditions, and in problems with the digestive system. A number of doctors also feel that difficult relationships can upset the natural immune system, making some patients more prone to attack by viruses, infectious diseases and conditions such as MS and ME. Dr W. Munro says, in his book Beat Stress, 'The psyche will often "dump" unresolved emotions and pain into the body when it is overloaded.'*

### Mental Damage

*Some psychiatrists believe the same factors can play a part in causing various types of depression, phobias, panic attacks, eating disorders and many other neuroses.*

### Spiritual Damage

*Jesus says that when we flatly refuse to forgive, we are cut off from God because he cannot:*

- *hear us when we pray (Mark 11:25)*
- *accept our worship (Matt. 5:23)*
- *forgive our sins (Matt. 6:14–15)*

*Not only can our spiritual growth and personal relationship with God be impeded in this life, but we could even be eternally damaged. Some theologians say that if we won't forgive we don't go to heaven, because we can't be forgiven ourselves. I don't know if they are right – I am not a theologian – but I wouldn't like to take the risk!*

*Forgiving is impossible for most of us, but Jesus would not have told us to do it unless he meant to help us! He said, 'With man this is impossible, but with God all things are possible' (Matt. 19:26, NIV). Jesus also said, 'Apart from me you can do nothing' (John 15:5, NIV). And St Paul declares, 'I can do everything through him who gives me strength' (Phil. 4:13, NIV).*

4

# LONELINESS AND ISOLATION

When people begin to emerge from the numb sensation of shock, one of the first feelings that can hit them is isolation – and it seems to recur relentlessly throughout the entire process of mending.

'I went back to work for the first time the other day . . . everyone was very friendly and I got through the day pretty well, but the thing I found so hard was the loneliness. Crazy! I was surrounded by so many people I knew well, yet I felt this overwhelming sense of being cut off and not part of them any more . . . trapped in my own little bubble of space.' That was part of a letter from a man whose wife had recently died.

It is easy to understand this lonely feeling when the person or people we want and need most are suddenly missing. A huge empty space is left where they ought to be. 'When I look beside me, I see that there is no one to help me, no one to protect me. No one cares for me,' was how King David described this sensation in Psalm 142 (v. 4, GNB).

One woman commented after her husband's funeral, 'Everyone was there. The whole family came to the funeral, and lots of old friends from way back. It was good to see them all, but I kept on thinking, "If only he was here with me – to share all this – so we could talk about it all tonight over hot drinks – laugh at all the funny little things." But he'll never be there beside me – ever again. I'll always have to face things alone from now on, won't I?'

Often a move can bring about feelings of loneliness and isolation: 'I

*When I lie down, I go to sleep in peace; you alone, O Lord, keep me perfectly safe. (Ps. 4:8, GNB)*

always thought, "How lovely to retire to a little cottage in the country." But I wasn't prepared for the abject loneliness. No bustling shops, all my church friends gone, no neighbours shouting at each other – it's so quiet I can't sleep!'

## They Can't Possibly Understand

Sometimes, though, this sense of loneliness does not have quite such an obvious cause. When we are facing personal devastation for whatever reason, we can feel surrounded by a swarm of well-wishers who all seem to say, 'I know just how you feel', but how can they? No one in all the history of the world has ever faced quite the same set of circumstances as you are facing now. You are unique. No one else thinks, acts and reacts just as you do. No one else's body feels pain in the same way as yours does. No one else can possibly get into your mind and see these events from your point of view. You really are alone in all this. Yet everyone you meet seems to have a nephew, a friend or a mother-in-law who has had exactly the same thing happen to them.

People always seem to know what you ought to do, and they make you feel even more isolated by their disapproval when you fail to take their unasked-for advice. They shower you with platitudes and send you cards with trite little messages written all over them. But they *don't understand*! 'My days have passed; my plans have failed; my hope is gone. But my friends say night is daylight; they say that light is near, but I know I remain in darkness' (Job 17:11–12, GNB) was how Job described this, and he certainly had a difficult time with his friends!

> *Whoever goes to the Lord for safety, whoever remains under the protection of the Almighty, can say to him, 'You are my defender and protector. You are my God; in you I trust.' . . . He will cover you with his wings, you will be safe in his care; his faithfulness will protect and defend you.* (Ps. 91:1–4, GNB)

## Embarrassment and Fear

There are other occasions when we could do with a few of these well-wishers back again, however irritating they may be:

'The first time I went out into the village after Bill died, it was terrible. People looked at me with frozen faces, not liking to smile or say anything. I suppose they must have felt embarrassed – not sure what to say, or frightened of saying the wrong thing. So they crossed over the road rather than meet me head on. Others hurried into shops or just looked the other way. I felt so utterly lonely that I didn't know what to do with myself. If only one of them had just come up and given me a hug.'

Another woman said: 'When our fourth baby was born with a hare-lip and cleft palate, it seemed so odd taking him out in the pram. With all the others it had been such fun pushing the new baby up to the school gate. Everyone came over to have a look, say nice things, and make cooing noises. But with Peter . . . no one came near us, it felt like being invisible.'

One woman who has had a stroke said: 'People are afraid of illness, I suppose. Steven pushes me out in the wheelchair to the shops sometimes, but neighbours often won't look at me or say "good morning" like they used to when I was well. They just talk to Steven. Perhaps they think, "If she can have a stroke at her age, I could have one too." The thought worries them so much they ignore it – and that means ignoring me as well.'

King David must also have felt like this: 'I had hoped for sympathy, but there was none; for comfort, but I found none' (Ps. 69:20, GNB).

## He Ought to Be Over It by Now!

Most 'spectators' do not understand just how long grieving takes. This is yet another cause of loneliness and misunderstanding.

> *You hold me by the hand . . . What else have I in heaven but you? Since I have you, what else could I want on earth? My mind and my body may grow weak, but God is my strength; he is all I ever need.* (Ps. 73:23–26, GNB)

'Everyone was round here like a swarm of bees at first,' one friend of mine told me. 'But I felt so dazed I didn't need them – in fact, I wished they'd go away. Once the numbness wore off I felt awful, and began to need them all badly, but by then they thought I ought to be getting over it and had drifted back to their own lives.'

## I Just Can't Face People

When Beattie was involved in a car crash on the motorway, the whole church seemed to rally around to support the family. After being discharged from hospital, she remembers how people were 'always popping round with flowers, cakes and even whole meals wrapped in tin foil. I felt so loved, but when at last I got the plaster off my legs, they couldn't understand why I didn't come back to church. I didn't know myself really – it sounded so silly to say I was too scared. There were other families in the church by that time who were going through the mill, and everyone's attention moved on to them. That was when I began to feel isolated and forgotten.

'Every Sunday I tried to go back, but the thought of all the smiling faces and the noisy chorus-singing frightened me. I felt I would panic if I was stuck in a crowd and couldn't get out if I wanted to. After a while, I began to feel I didn't dare come out of my house at all; I felt safe inside, but couldn't cope with big shops and lots of people.

'I missed my friends at church so much, but they soon forget you if you don't show up on a Sunday, so I began to feel cross with them all – kind of bitter and hurt inside. I thought they couldn't be bothered and didn't care any more. The gap got wider and wider until I didn't *want* to see them. I turned in on myself, I suppose, and got very depressed and weepy.

'When I went to the hospital for my check-up I mentioned this fear of being with people, and I was so relieved when the doctor said it was entirely normal and a symptom of Post Traumatic Stress.

' "It will pass," he told me, "but it may take you two years to become desensitised." Actually, it didn't take more than a few weeks, because once I knew the feeling had a medical explanation and

*And I will be with you always, to the end of the age.* (Matt. 28:20, GNB)

wasn't just me being silly, I was able to ask one of the pastoral team to come round and pray with me about it. His wife helped me so much that first day I dared to go back – she walked in with me and we sat together. After that day, I gradually began to get back into the life of church again. Just knowing that my feelings were normal helped me turn the corner.'

## A New Dimension

When we feel our lives have stopped completely, we often find it hard to realise that the rest of the world is still whizzing on just the same as ever. The following comments illustrate this:

'I heard someone laughing in the hospital corridor outside my room, and I thought, "How can people still laugh?" Then I thought, "But why shouldn't they, it's just another Tuesday morning for them".'

'I looked out of the window and saw people hurrying off to catch the London train or walking their dogs, and I thought, "How can they, when Brian is dead?"'

'At first I felt like a car, broken down on a motorway. Shunted on to the hard shoulder while everyone else went driving along at high speed, bound for exciting places to do important things, leaving me behind and forgotten.'

Traumatic experiences change values, and turn priorities on their heads. In fact, they actually move us as people into a new dimension, so that a lot of the people who used to travel comfortably through life with us are suddenly left behind. Their interests and involvements seem oddly trivial and childish.

On several occasions during the eight years that I was ill, my condition became life threatening, and I had to be hastily admitted to hospital. While this was very hard on my children, I do think it

---

*Jesus said, 'A time is coming ... when you will be scattered ... You will leave me all alone. Yet I am not alone, for my Father is with me.' (John 16:32, NIV)*

helped them develop a very sound set of values. One of our daughters was fourteen during one of my acute episodes. One day, when she came home from school, she threw her bag down on the kitchen table with rather more force than was usual for a gentle character like her.

'What's up?' Tony enquired.

'It's spots!' she said crossly. 'All they can talk about is *spots*! But what do little things like that matter when Mum might be dead by tomorrow?'

## Self-imposed Isolation

Recently, I was on my way to speak at a coffee morning in a Baptist church, and I took Brodie, my dog, to keep me company in the car. We arrived early, so I took her into a nearby park for a walk and there I met a young woman who also had a black labrador. Dog-lovers never wait to be introduced, and soon we were chatting away. I explained where I was going and asked if she knew the church. She looked as if she was going to cry as she replied, 'I used to go there – but I can't any more.' She went on to tell me about a terrible day, two years before, when she had lost her temper and battered her small son very badly. 'I knocked his front teeth out by banging his face against the banisters. My husband had just left me and I was at the end of my tether, but I never should have hurt my son like that. He looked terrible, and of course everyone kept asking him what had happened. I was so ashamed that I never went back to church again. I keep away from all my other friends too. I don't feel I deserve to have company after that.'

We sat down on a bench and talked about forgiveness for so long that I was nearly late for the coffee morning! The best bit of this story is that she came along to it with me, and received such a warm welcome that she has been going every week since.

## Invisible Walls of Protection

When I spoke about loneliness at a ladies' conference once, a girl called Barbara was talking to me at the end when she suddenly burst into tears.

---

*Thy presence fills my solitude.* (Longfellow)

'I've been a loner for a long time now,' she told me. 'But really I can't think why – I never used to be like this. I go to a good church and I'm reasonably happy in my job.'

After we had prayed and asked the Lord Jesus to show us the cause of her isolation, she began to tell me about something that had happened to her four years before.

'I don't really want to talk about it,' she admitted. 'In fact, I've never told anyone else.' She had been on holiday in Tenerife when one night she had been attacked and raped by a stranger in the hotel car park. 'I never went to the police. I felt so degraded, so ashamed. I was a virgin, you see, and I felt as if I had lost something precious. Somehow, I got myself back to my room. All I wanted to do was have a bath and get clean again – or try to, anyway. I don't think I've ever really felt clean since. It's stupid, I know, but I can't stop myself from feeling guilty – as if it was my fault. The others on the holiday with me just thought I was ill in bed with a tummy bug for the next few days, and I felt too ashamed to tell them because we were all from the same church.

'As I was flying home, I decided to leave the whole thing behind me and never think of it again. But ever since, I've had an odd feeling of being cut off – even from myself – sort of shut in behind walls. My Christian life's gone dead on me too, and I feel distant in all my relationships. There's a really nice boy at church who wants us to get serious, but I can't seem to make a commitment somehow.'

We prayed together, and then I explained that when we are hurt we often build invisible walls round ourselves for a while as a kind of protection.

'I know I've done that,' she said tearfully, 'but I don't know how to take them down again.'

'You could ask Jesus to do it for you,' I suggested. 'Sometimes he has to demolish these protective walls before he can begin rebuilding our broken lives.'

'But I'm not really sure I want him to demolish them,' she replied uneasily. 'I would feel so exposed, and I've got used to hiding the real me from people now.'

'But Jesus would never do anything suddenly and brutally, like a demolition gang moving in with grappling irons and dynamite,' I

*With my God I can scale a wall.* (Ps. 18:29, NIV)

assured her. 'When we put him in control of the mending operations, he actually builds his own wall of protection round us *before* he starts dismantling our own walls. Then he usually works away on us very slowly and gently. In fact, he will melt your walls away gradually by his love. The more you expose yourself to that love, the more he will be able to do for you.'

A look of sheer relief began to spread over Barbara's face. I can't say she went home radiant and instantly healed of her problems – she did not. For months, she regularly visited a Christian counsellor who was able to help her gradually forgive the man who had attacked her, but the moment when her ultimate healing began was when she gave the Lord permission to come inside her lonely sanctuary.

## Beware of the 'Hold Up' Factor

The invisible walls we construct to keep out other people can be a safe retreat while we are vulnerable emotionally, but we can become permanent prisoners in our own fortress unless at some point we deliberately decide to come out and start relating to others normally again.

There are all kinds of colourful examples of this 'hold up' factor in fiction. Silas Marner, in George Eliot's book of that name, felt so hurt by his church community that he went off alone and lived as a recluse in an isolated cottage. Miss Haversham of Great Expectations is Charles Dickens's version of the same phenomenon. She remained alone after being jilted on her wedding day, cut off from the world by echoing corridors and locked doors, while her wedding finery decayed around her.

The danger of this lonely stage is that when the people who once filled our world have suddenly gone, we feel so devastated that we never make new contacts. It either seems too much of an effort to make new friendships, or we fail to get close to new people because we stubbornly refuse to let go of people we have lost.

> *Sometimes He takes away that which is most precious so that into the void of a life that is utterly broken He may pour the glory of his indwelling love.* (Dr Alan Redpath)

### People Need People – Even the Shy Ones

Hiding away in isolation for too long can be dangerous for many reasons, but one of them is that we need a 'dustbin' for our 'rubbish'! Talking to someone who really cares is a wonderful way of getting rid of painful feelings, and can be tremendously healing. However close God may seem when we are distressed, we also badly need human beings to listen to us as well. Perhaps Jesus comes to us most easily wearing the body of an ordinary person. Once, when my oldest son Justyn was only five and not very happy at school, I went to meet him. He trailed across the playground towards me, his little, white, tear-stained face looking up at me pathetically from the hood of his grey duffel coat.

'Whatever went wrong, darling?' I asked him.

'Everything,' was his tragic reply. 'My sums wouldn't come right, the teacher was cross, and no one loved me all day.'

'That's not true,' said his six-year-old sister reproachfully. 'Jesus loves you, and he's with you – even in the toilet.'

'Yes, but Jesus doesn't have arms these days to cuddle sad people,' was Justyn's profound reply.


### *Warning!*

It is very hard to find the right person on whom to dump our emotions. We begin to remove a brick or two of our protective wall when we think we can trust someone, but then suddenly we realise they are looking at us blankly or even with a hint of contempt, so we hastily build the wall back up again and pin back the smile that says 'I'm fine'. The next time someone comes close enough to talk, we feel too vulnerable to risk it. We need to find someone who will not:

- crush us or make us feel silly
- bombard us with good advice
- listen to all we say, and then relate it to everyone else at church under the guise of 'a prayer topic'
- rush us through the mending process too quickly

---

*In a desert land he found him, in a barren and howling waste. He shielded him and cared for him; he guarded him as the apple of his eye. (Deut. 32:10, NIV)*

---

- stop us from moving forward (there are people who will want to wrap us up in cottonwool sympathy, keeping us prisoners to their own need to be needed)

We need someone who will listen to us, accept us as we are at this moment, and walk beside us without condemnation. People like that are rare, and during the eight years I was ill I made some bad mistakes until I specifically asked God to send me the right person at the right time. I soon discovered he had the remarkable knack of bringing along human 'arms' whenever he saw that I needed a metaphorical cuddle. Perhaps it is far safer to leave the choice of our friend and confidant to God rather than blundering up to the wrong person and being hurt yet again.

## The Challenge

Someone once said, 'Loss is inevitable, but growth is optional.' It sounds very irritating, but it does happen to be true. Each of the stages in the Broken Teapot Syndrome faces us with a challenge: we can use it to help us move on in our growth towards God, or we can refuse the jump like a horse in the show ring. The questions the Lord asks us in our isolation are:

- 'Will you exclude me as well as everyone else?'
- 'Will you allow me to come in and fill your emptiness?'
- 'Can I be the friend and companion you need so badly just now?'

Perhaps the day when I felt most abandoned and lonely was also the day when I allowed him to come to me through my own invisible wall. I have written about this before, in *Unexpected Healing*, but the moment was so special that I make no apologies for telling the story again. It was just over two years after I first became ill, and soon after I had fallen in the cow dung. We were on holiday in Yorkshire, and one day Tony took the children off for a long hike over the moors, leaving me alone in the car park.

No-one came to my support, but everyone deserted me. May it not be held against them. But the Lord stood at my side and gave me strength. (2 Tim. 4:16, 17, NIV)

'You'll be all right, won't you, Mum?' they said, as they settled me in the wheelchair with a little rug over my knees like an old granny. 'I will,' I lied, forcing myself to sound cheerful, but as I watched them walking away up the path to the moors my smile slipped away and the tears took its place. Other families were also eagerly setting out for a day's hiking, and the empty car park felt very bleak indeed. By that time, I was beginning to get used to expressing my feelings to God, so I said to him, 'I could have done so much for you, if only you'd heard all those prayers and healed me.'

I *felt* (rather than heard) his reply: 'Lots of people are willing to *do* things for me, but not many are willing to be my friends, and that is what I want most of all.'

That single fact was probably the most important thing I learnt in all those eight years of illness. We ourselves – our friendship and company – are far more valuable to God than any service we could ever render to him. Yet so often, when our 'Teapots' are smashed, the greatest distress we experience is *not* being able to do all that we once thought was important. We value ourselves by what we can achieve, so when the power to 'produce results' is taken from us, we feel worthless, useless and fit for the scrap heap. God values us not for our achievements, but for ourselves and for our company. We are so valuable to Jesus that he gave up everything he had to win our friendship – his life in heaven, and then his life on earth.

Most friends expect a measure of give-and-take in relationships, and that is why so many of the less faithful ones back away when we do not seem to be 'mending' as quickly as they feel we should. Their motives for being our friends are, to a certain extent, selfish. Morever, the kind of friendship that Jesus offers to us is utterly unselfish. He is willing to hang in there with us, however long this mending process takes, however difficult we are to live with, and however violently we express our reactions. He is always there, night or day; he never gets bored with the same old stuff coming up over and over again, and he always understands us completely.

Out of the terrible feeling of isolation I felt that day in Yorkshire came the discovery that God was my friend. If that love relationship of trust and intimate friendship is actually the most important thing

---

*A man of many companions may come to ruin, but there is a friend who sticks closer than a brother.* (Prov. 18:24, NIV)

any human being can acquire then anything that helps us towards that goal is good. So whenever we feel that lonely, empty, lost feeling creeping up on us, if we form the habit of turning to Jesus and asking him to fill our solitude with himself, then even our most unpleasant experiences can become our greatest blessings.

## A Meditation

She stood alone, waiting, as the evening shadows gathered around her. She was always waiting these days; and she was always alone. People were hurrying and bustling all around her, but they did not seem to notice her standing there, separated from the rest of the world, isolated by shame. Women were on their way home from the well to cook their husbands' food, but she had no husband and often these days she had no food either. The men were closing up their market stalls, calling to each other as they finished their day's work, but she had no work, except this, and now she was getting older even the other street women excluded her from their company.

She stepped back further into the shadows. Dim light was her only hope of bread tomorrow – it hid her greying hair and the wrinkles round her eyes. Fortunately, soldiers were not fussy – and this was a garrison town. She shuddered as a wave of utter degradation swept over her. What a way to earn her bread, selling her body to Gentile pigs.

It had been one of them who had started it all, long ago when she was a young girl, happy and carefree in this very marketplace. He had walked by, his helmet flashing in the sunshine, and she had loved him. Yes, that was the beginning of her shame, and now at the end of it all she could never undo her mistake and start again. Righteous people never forgive, and this town was full of righteous people.

A group of men were coming down the road. Suddenly alert, she stepped forward to take a closer look, but their clothes were dusty from the journey and very shabby. Men like that had no money to spare, and she sighed, for she was hungry. Perhaps she should try anyway? You could never tell, and the evening light was kinder now, so she let her shawl slip from her long, unbraided hair and stepped out into their path.

She had done it a thousand times before, but still she hated it. She had been kicked into the gutter too many times by righteous men, and felt the blows from their sticks. Of course, the Pharisees never hit her; they would not defile themselves by touching an outcast like her, but the disdain in their faces as they turned away hurt far more than any blow. Were these men righteous, she wondered.

The leader stopped. Perhaps he was a customer? She looked up into his face, expecting to see the usual greedy glance of appraisal, but instead she encountered an expression she had never seen on anyone's face before. This man neither despised her nor wished to use her. In fact, his smile gave her the strange feeling that she was loved – really loved for the very first time in her life.

They stood there in the busy roadway for a long time, and somehow she felt his eyes were looking right into her soul, reading all the degradation and disgrace, but without condemnation. Then at last he put out his hand and gently touched her shoulder. It was only a simple gesture, but it made her feel that, in spite of knowing everything she had ever done wrong, she was still deemed valuable – and that it might, even now, be possible to begin again.

'You are forgiven,' he said softly. 'Your shame is covered, your past is wiped clean.'

Then he was gone. Bemused and dizzy, she stood gazing after him. 'Who was that man?' she asked, grabbing the coat sleeve of one of his followers.

'That was Jesus,' he replied simply. 'The Messiah himself.' She gasped.

'Then he really can forgive sins,' she whispered. 'Am I really free at last?'

All through the evening she searched for him, up and down the little streets and alleyways, but no one would tell her where the strangers had gone, and they laughed at her scornfully.

'That Jesus is a righteous man,' they said. 'What would he want with a woman like you?'

She was almost desperate – what if he had left the town before she could give her gift to him? The tears were running down her painted cheeks as she stumbled along clutching her precious bundle. She had to find him. Suddenly, a child's footsteps came pattering up the street behind her.

'Hey, you!' he shouted cheekily. 'I know where he is, that man you want.' She turned suddenly, her heart beating wildly. 'He's at supper with Simon the Pharisee,' and he added with a mocking laugh, 'but you won't be welcome there!'

The child was right, of course. She had suffered more from Simon than any other man in town. He would not even allow her shadow to contaminate him, and his righteous indignation had caused him to make her a public example in the marketplace on several painful occasions. Of course, she ought to have realised that the Messiah would want to spend his time with people like Simon, men who had never sinned. Yet the man who had smiled at her today was not like Simon at all. There was acceptance and warmth in that smile, not contempt. And the memory of his smile gave her the courage to go to him.

It was not difficult to slip unnoticed into the house and across the courtyard; the servants were too busy with the meal to notice her. The drone of conversation came from a room where the lamplight flickered warm and inviting, and through the arches she could see men reclining on couches around the table. He was there all right, but she sensed at once that he was uncomfortable. His feet were still caked with the grime of his journey, and dust powdered his hair and beard. What were those servants thinking about, to insult a guest by not offering him water for washing, or oil for his head?

She crept closer; she must make him look in her direction before she was discovered, and the shouts and blows began. Respectable people like Simon would not tolerate an outcast defiling their home. The Pharisees, though, were so busy arguing about theology that they did not notice her as she slid to her knees at the foot of their visitor's couch.

From under her cloak, she took out the present. It was not much to give the Son of God himself, just a jar of scent, but it was all she had in the world. She had been saving it as a nest egg to keep her from starvation when she got too old to . . . work. Now she wanted to give him everything she had, holding nothing back for herself.

As she watched him, the tears began again: tears of sadness for a whole life thrown away; tears of repentance for the other lives she had ruined through her trade; tears of relief, too, that at last the terrible weight of guilt had gone for ever. They splashed down on to his dusty feet, and in her embarrassment she quickly wiped them away with her hair, hoping he would not notice.

But of course he did notice – and looking round, smiled at her again. He did not need to speak; she knew that to him she was not an outcast, excluded and alone. She could walk away from her past and live again, because at last she had found someone who could remove her shame. Such a surge of relief swept through her, followed by such an overwhelming sense of love, in that moment she determined in her heart to serve this man-shaped God for the rest of her life. What, though, could she possibly do for him?

Then she remembered his feet. She could at least take away the insult Simon had dealt him by washing them for him. As she broke the seal from her jar and let the valuable perfume trickle away, the pungent scent filled the house with its sweetness. The Pharisees looked around startled. There was a stunned silence as they saw her kneeling there, followed by a rumble of disapproval. 'Fancy letting a woman like that actually *touch* him!' said one in disgust.

Jesus looked round at them, and sadly shook his head. 'You think you are righteous,' he said, 'But you are caught by the most deadly sin, pride, which tells you that you have never sinned at all. Yes, this woman has sinned greatly, but she is forgiven. Do you see how she loves me? Her love is so great that it has transformed her life. She loves much because she has been forgiven much. Those who feel they have no need of forgiveness can never love like that.'

## A Prayer

*'Come to me, all you who are tired from carrying a heavy burden of loneliness . . . "for I will never leave you; I will never abandon you".'* (Heb. 13:5, GNB)

Yes, Lord Jesus, I do feel lonely. Most of what I valued is gone. Loss seems to surround me like a great wide ocean, leaving me cut off on an island, quite alone. Loss on all sides, loss in every direction, loss, loss, loss as far as the eye can see. All I can hear are the echoes of familiar voices and laughter from the past, and all my hopes and desires lie shipwrecked on the rocks around my island. The memories of all the things I wanted to do, places I wanted to visit, people I wanted to meet, merely mock me now that I am stranded here in this desolate place.

No one else knows I'm lonely. People can't see it by looking at me

---

*I will not leave you as orphans; I will come to you.* (John 14:18, NIV)

from the outside. How could they ever understand unless they had been there themselves? But you have. You must have been lonely so often, because the people you loved best always seemed to misunderstand what you said and did. That night in the garden when you faced the worst ordeal of your life, you desperately needed your three best friends to be there for you, but they let you down and went to sleep. They couldn't come with you into your private anguish, and when the soldiers came to torture and kill you, they ran for their lives.

So, because you understand, will you come into my loneliness and share it with me? Then, because I know I am not alone after all, please give me the courage to stop excluding other people. They could be the very ones you might be sending to me, friends who are willing to be your arms to comfort me, your mind to understand me, your hands to hold mine and steady me, your smile to reassure me, your voice of compassion. Please breathe on these separating walls and begin to melt them away. Yet, Lord, I am so afraid of being exposed to the world out there; please help me.

## Perhaps the Lord Would Respond Like This

'Do not fear, for I am with you; do not be dismayed, for I am your God. I will strengthen you and help you; I will uphold you with my righteous right hand' (Isa. 41:10, NIV).

## STOP FOR A MOMENT

*During the mending process it can be dangerous to make major moves or changes that you might regret when you finally emerge with a new, reshaped 'teapot'. Right now, you cannot trust your feelings, and one day you may wish that:*

Fear *had not made you leave your job now that you feel more confident and able to cope again.*

Isolation *had not made you choose to move to that cottage in the wilds, now that you want to be near people again and are sick of being a hermit.*

Anger *had not made you leave your church and resign from that committee, or get out of teaching for good.*

Loneliness *had not rushed you into making a relationship that you now find is a disaster.*

Denial *had not made you suppress your righteous anger so that you accepted a compromise and left someone who depends on you to suffer the consequences.*

Depression, *causing a temporary loss of faith, had not caused you to resign from your ministry.*

Painful feelings *had not made you walk out on your marriage before giving God a chance to help you work through your feelings.*

Guilt *(the false kind) had not made you feel so worthless that you gave up being a housegroup leader or Sunday School teacher.*

*You need to let the mending process happen gradually, until you find the 'new you' at the far end, then make any life-changing decisions. Of course, some decisions have to be made quickly, but God really can be trusted to help you make the right ones. We just tend to sit and wait for a voice to boom at us from the skies above. Yet God does not seem to do that. He seems to guide us while we are on the move, but we can always trust him to stop us from doing the wrong thing. We take a step in one direction, and if he does not block our progress we continue walking along that road. If, however, we do hit a barrier, then we should change direction until we find a clear path to follow.*
*'If you wander off the road to the right or the left, you will hear his voice behind you saying, "Here is the road. Follow it"' (Isa. 30:21, GNB).*

# 5

# FEAR

Fear, anxiety and worry are all very predictable reactions when our 'teapots' are smashed, and their causes are easy to find:

'I hate the dark. Now I'm alone in the house at night, I'm too afraid to sleep.' Being alone is a very common cause of fear, and so is the feeling of not being able to cope.

'John did everything for me, sorted out the mortgage, income tax, the bills. He made all the decisions, and he could mend anything from a hole in the roof to a dripping tap. Now that he's gone, I just don't know how to cope with it all, and I feel worried all the time.'

Some people say they feel all right during the day, but wake up at about three in the morning in a cold sweat, and start on the 'What if . . . ?' cycle:

- What if I can't make it on my own?
- What if I can't get a job?
- What if the children get out of hand without a father's control?
- What if the finances don't work out?
- What if I get too lonely to face life at all?

## Reactions to Fear

### In illness and pain

The following comments are typical of the fear that people experience concerning illness:

'I feel very positive most of the time since finding out I've got cancer, but then I suddenly think, "Suppose the doctors aren't telling me everything." Then I start wondering if the next scan will show it's reached the liver, and how much longer I would have. I usually wind up getting so worried that they won't give me enough pain control that I have to take something for my headache!'

'Mostly I can cope with this disease and the irritating disabilities it causes, but I know it's progressive, and I'm so afraid that one day I'll be trapped inside myself, not able to speak or move at all.'

'I'd willingly go through this myself; it's watching my child suffering that terrifies me so much – and the constant anxiety that we might lose him.'

### A loss of identity

'I don't know who I am any more. All the little things that made up my life have gone: the ordinary everyday routines, activities and responsibilities, my role and position in the "pecking order" of life, all the people I met every day and worked beside – they were my props and I've lost them all. I feel as if I'm walking off the edge of a cliff into nothingness. The uncertainty terrifies me.'

### It can come in 'monster' waves

'If I go out to the shops I get these terrible panic attacks. My heart begins to pound, and I hear rushing noises in my head. I'm too afraid to move in any direction, I feel like I'm choking, and I get this awful pain in my chest. The first time it happened I thought I was having a heart attack and was going to die on the spot.'

### It can be milder, but continuous

'It's always there just under the surface. I don't suppose I look worried; people wouldn't guess if they meet me out in the street, but I'm constantly tense and edgy. And I get butterflies in the tummy nearly all the time.'

---

*He did not promise to take from our paths the events that we fear, but he did promise to take away from us the fear of those events.* (Tom Rees)

### It can paralyse us

'Recently I've begun to feel that I can't face people; I can't think what to say, and I'm afraid they'll discover just what a wreck I've become, so when I hear the doorbell ring, I freeze. I just can't open the door, so I sit quiet and hope they think I'm out.'

### It can make us run

'I was walking down the High Street when I saw someone from our old church coming towards me – one of the people who'd been so critical and beastly before we left. I turned tail and pelted down a side street. She must have seen me, and I felt such a fool, but I was just too scared to meet her again.'

## The Plight of the Earwig

Most human beings fear change – it threatens us. Change, even change for the better, makes us feel unsettled and insecure. It is not surprising that we often feel afraid during this mending process, because it is really a journey through change. At the beginning, Granny's teapot stood perfect behind the glass doors of her display cabinet; at the other end of the change process, it had become a fascinating plant holder on the window ledge. There would have been a time in between those two points when the half-mended teapot was neither one thing or the other, because it was in the middle of being changed. A person in this state can look back at the life he or she once had and feel separated from it, but the life still to be lived is shrouded in uncertainty because the person has not arrived there yet. So there is a nasty sensation of not belonging anywhere – and that is very frightening. I remember going to our housegroup one evening when I was feeling exactly like that, and someone quoted a saying of Cardinal Newman. It did not help me at all, and it probably won't help you either! But here it is anyway:

> *When we walk in the shadow of his protection nothing can ever harm us again. They may hurt us but they can never crush or destroy us for we are always safe when we walk with him.* (Tom Rees)

'To live is to grow,
to grow is to change.
So to live successfully is to change often.'

The very thought that God might be developing us into a new kind of person is frightening. Most of us were perfectly happy as we were – we felt safe in the old familiar rut of long-held attitudes, thought patterns and routines. Caught in the middle of the process of change, we feel as vulnerable as an earwig when changing its skin. The earwig carries its skeleton on the outside, so its body can only enlarge during the few hours when its hard outer layer has been shed and the new, soft exterior is in the process of hardening. Naturally, the earwig is very vulnerable indeed during these times, a prey to any greedy blackbird. It can't feel safe until its soft white skin has become brown and hardened into a new outer shell. Sudden change often makes we humans feel the same!

## The Challenge

This fear is perfectly normal – but for Christians it poses a problem. The Bible says 'Fear not', at least 365 times, and we are also told, 'Don't give in to worry . . . it only leads to trouble' (Ps. 37:8, GNB). So are we being sinful and letting the Lord down when we feel anxious? Once again, let's remember that just because we are Christian, we do not stop being human. Human beings suffer from stress when their security is threatened, and stress pumps into the bloodstream the 'fight or flight' chemicals that saved our ancestors from sabre-toothed tigers. When we are stuck in a situation we cannot fight, flight is our only option, and therefore fear is both natural and inevitable. It is what we do with the fear that matters. Will we let it destroy us or work for us?

There are possibly two questions that the Lord is asking when fear

*Do not cling to events of the past or dwell on what happened long ago. Watch for the new thing I am going to do. It is happening already – you can see it now! I will make a road through the wilderness and give you streams of water there.* (Isa. 43:18–19, GNB)

shakes and rattles the half-mended pieces of 'teapot', and the first one is:

● 'Do you believe I have the power to keep you safe?'

As I said in Chapter 3, fear has always been an enemy of mine. Once, when so many things were going wrong for us that I felt terrified of what might happen next, I went to have coffee with a friend of mine. On her sitting-room floor stood an old wire birdcage, and prowling all round it were seven kittens. They were so big they were really cats, but I guessed they looked like tigers to the occupant of the cage! They hissed maliciously through the bars with obvious evil intent, and clawed viciously at the door catch. Guessing the poor little bird must be scared to pulp, I stepped in among those savage monsters to take a closer look, but the perch was empty and there was no sign of a bird in the cage. Instead, I saw a cheeky little hamster lying on his back in a bed of cotton wool, contentedly nibbling a peanut. Now and again he looked up at those claws and teeth as if to say, 'I know my owner cares enough about me to make sure those bars are strong enough for my protection – so I'm going to enjoy this nut and say nuts to you!' I prayed that the Lord would give me as much faith as the hamster, and went home feeling considerably better.

The second question is:

● 'Do you believe I am speaking the truth when I say, "Do not be afraid – I will save you. I have called you by name – you are mine"?' (Isa. 43:1, GNB.)

Most of us would reply promptly, 'Yes, of course I believe all that,' but at the very back of our minds there is often a tiny seed of doubt. Many of us have rather an abstract, academic or secondhand kind of faith. When we are fit, earning a good salary, and surrounded by people who love us, we can go to church and sing loudly about Jesus meeting all our needs, but how can we know for sure that he really will – until the crunch comes and our faith is put to the test?

At the start of any airline flight the airhostess always stands at the

*How I plead with God, how I implore his mercy, pouring out my troubles before him. For I am overwhelmed and desperate, and you alone know which way I ought to turn.* (Ps. 142:1–3, LB)

front of the cabin and tells everyone what to do if the plane should crash. No one ever seems to listen as she points out the emergency exits and models the lifejacket. People sit nonchalantly reading their newspapers, but do those passengers ever think, 'I wonder if that little bit of orange plastic she's waving about would *really* hold me up if this plane came down in the sea? Would it *really* inflate on impact as she says it would?' Well, of course they can't be sure until that 'unlikely event' actually occurs. Yet surely it is when our lives are crashing and our faith is put under pressure, that we are forced to ask, 'Is it *really* going to work?'

Because Jesus loves us so completely, he longs for us to trust him to look after us in every way. In fact, we are insulting him when we say we love him without also trusting him. Peter tells us that our faith is more precious to God than gold (1 Pet. 1:7), and without it we cannot please him (Heb. 11:6). It is that implicit, hamster-like trust that he wants to develop in us during this stage of the Broken Teapot Syndrome.

When my friend Trisha discovered she had multiple sclerosis, her husband walked out and left her prey to all kinds of anxieties. 'It seemed so unfair,' she told me. 'I could just about understand that he couldn't cope with illness and didn't want to see me gradually deteriorating, but you would think the least he could do was to see I was all right financially.' He was late with her maintenance cheques every time, leaving her sick with worry over the unpaid bills. In the end, he stopped sending anything at all and she had to take him to court.

'The whole thing was a constant nightmare,' said Trisha. 'I was forced to put the house on the market because the MS was making it impossible to live with so many stairs. Yet my husband demanded his share of the sale, so I knew I wouldn't be able to afford a bungalow – they always seem more expensive. I just didn't know what I was going to do, and I felt absolutely beside myself with worry.

---

*I alone know the plans I have for you, plans to bring you prosperity and not disaster, plans to bring about the future you hope for. Then you will call to me. You will come and pray to me, and I will answer you. You will seek me, and you will find me because you will seek me with all your heart.* (Jer. 29:11–13, GNB)

'Then one day I felt "confronted" by the Lord. He seemed to say to me, "Are you looking to *me* to sort your finances out, or to Terry?" I had to admit that I felt it was my husband's obligation to look after me – after all, I was his responsibility, the courts had said so. He jolly well owed it to me after walking out just because I became ill. But then I realised that the Lord wanted to be "my provider", to take the responsibility of my care and maintenance, just as if he had become my husband. I did have to struggle with that, but in the end it was a very important part of my being able to forgive Terry for rejecting me. (That was something I was working through at that time.) Letting him off the debt I felt he owed me helped me to let go of all the bitterness and resentment I had been feeling towards him. I made a definite decision to rely on the Lord in the future. If he wanted to meet my needs through Terry, well, that was fine, but if he wanted to use some other way, that was fine too. I stopped nagging his solicitor when cheques failed to arrive, or writing abusing letters to Terry or screaming at him down the phone. Whenever some emergency arose, I just said, "Lord, what are you going to do now?" And somehow the needs were always met.

'Mind you, they weren't always met instantly! I sweated a bit when I finally sold the house and had about six weeks to get out and nowhere to go. The council wouldn't give me a flat because Terry was supposed to provide me with a home, but of course he wouldn't give me enough to buy something suitable for my disability. I was desperate, and wondered what on earth the Lord would do about it. Then, most unexpectedly, I heard that an aunt of mine who had recently died had left me her bungalow. It was on the other side of town, but my mobility allowance came through just then, so I could get an adapted car that made it still possible to get back to see my beloved friends at church. A lot needed doing to the bungalow, but I lived there in the meantime, and the money Terry finally gave me was enough to pay for everything to be made easy for me as a disabled person. Now my favourite verse is Philippians 4:19 (NIV): "My God will meet all your needs according to his glorious riches in Christ Jesus." '

---

*The Lord himself will lead you and be with you. He will not fail you or abandon you, so do not lose courage or be afraid.* (Deut.31:8, GNB)

When, like Trisha, everything and everyone who represents safety and security in our lives is removed, and we have no way of meeting our own necessities any more, our need for God is paramount, and that is when we really discover for sure that we can trust him.

## Doesn't God Want Me to Be Mature and Self-reliant?

One day Jesus startled a group of confident, well-qualified men by telling them he wanted them to become like small children again. They had been arguing for hours about which of them had the most to offer the new Kingdom they thought Jesus was about to set up in Jerusalem: which of them would make the best Prime Minister, and who should manage the finances. They all thought they had abilities and personal qualities that Jesus could use to meet the needs of his Kingdom, but before he could use any of them they had to learn to trust him.

Some commentators say Peter's own little son was the child Jesus called, and, lifting him up on to his knee, he said to those big, proud, self-confident men something like this: 'Until you recognise you are as helpless and dependent as this child you can never be important in my kingdom' (Matt. 18:3-4, paraphrased).

## God Brings His Children up Backwards

When I was expecting our first child, Sarah, I used to love feeling her kicking round inside me. She was totally dependent on me to meet her every need, and she belonged to me completely. The moment she took her first gasp of breath and the midwife cut the cord, I had to begin letting her go. Our assignment as earthly parents was to turn this totally dependent scrap of humanity into a self-sufficient adult who could function without any help from us whatsoever.

The first steps towards this goal were a delight to us. One day, as we pushed cereal into her mouth, she grabbed the spoon and shoved it into her ear – or was it up her nose?

*When anxiety was great within me, your consolation brought joy to my soul.* (Ps. 94:19, NIV)

'Oh look!' we cried in wonder, 'she's feeding herself!'

When she took her first tottering step we rang all our friends and exclaimed proudly, 'She's walking – already!'

Then the really big day came: she used her potty. I was so thrilled with her sheer cleverness that I felt like showing the contents to the milkman!

It hurt like mad to hand her over to the teacher on her first day at school, but I knew I had to let go if we were ever to achieve the goal of her independence. From that time on, the steps she took away from us gradually lengthened, and we watched with pride as we taught her to meet her own needs instead of always looking to us to meet them for her.

'If you want money, you earn it,' we said, as we sent her off in a heatwave or a thunderstorm to pick fruit on the local farm.

And finally, we accompanied her to her chosen university, and had to watch her walk away into the huge building while we travelled home in desolation without her. She soon came back again, of course – along with her dirty washing! It was not until she had her own home and career that we knew we had finally launched her into the world as an independent adult, able to earn her own living and solve her own problems.

God works backwards. Usually by the time he becomes our Father, we have already become self-sufficient adults. God knows that in this universe our only hope of true and lasting happiness is to depend on him entirely. Trusting in ourselves and our own abilities may sound very 'manly' and adult, but it is actually a recipe for disaster on this dark planet. We are not the giants we think we are, and God never designed us to live without him.

So he has to work on us – backwards – gently dismantling each of our little self-sufficiencies and allowing our earthly props to be removed. His ultimate aim is for us to depend on him for everything, just as Sarah depended on me during those nine months in the womb. St Paul describes this by saying, 'In him we live and move and have our being . . . We are his offspring' (Acts 17:28, NIV). Only when we reach this state of utter dependency, and are fully under his control, can we safely function in this world. The Broken Teapot

---

*His never-failing love protects me like the walls of a fort!*
(Ps. 31:21, LB)

Syndrome may feel to us like a catastrophe, but it could have huge potential in God's eyes, because, as Sören Kierkegaard said, 'God created everything out of nothing and everything which God is to use he first reduces to nothing.'

King David was one of the greatest soldiers and statesmen who ever lived, and the stories of his achievements still ring triumphantly down through the years. Yet his secret was this utter dependence on God; and, except for two unfortunate occasions, he never made a decision without first turning to God for his guidance. Towards the end of his life he wrote, 'My heart is not proud, O Lord . . . I do not concern myself with great matters or things too wonderful for me. But I have stilled and quietened my soul; like a weaned child with its mother, like a weaned child is my soul within me' (Ps. 131:1–2, NIV).

## Lost in the Forest

Like many babies born in the war, I did not see much of my father during the first few years of my life. And when he did come home, he didn't have very much to do with me.

'Babies are noisy, smelly creatures that ruin everything,' was the way he described me in his diary. My noises and smells were left to my nanny to cope with, and he and I hardly coincided at all until the day he offered to buy me an icecream. I must have been about three, and my mother and I were staying in my grandparents' house in Scotland. My father arrived to spend a few days with us, and he obviously felt it was time I had some paternal contact.

My reactions to his overture of friendship were mixed. Icecreams were a rare treat in those days of rationing, but they could only be bought in a shop in the next village – a long walk away. (Petrol was rationed, too.) Could I really dare to go off alone with this big, remote stranger with the loud, deep voice? However, greed overcame fear and I opted for the icecream. We set off, walking stiffly and silently down the path by the sea.

It was about three o'clock on an October afternoon and the light already seemed to be failing. 'You can't walk very fast, can you?' my

*Cast all your anxiety on him because he cares for you.* (1 Pet. 5:7, NIV)

father commented, as my short legs tried to keep pace with his long strides. 'I think we'll take the short cut through the forest or we'll never get there before dark.'

The forest! Terror seized me. All my bedtime stories seemed to contain wolves and trolls who lived in forests. I had never been in one, but I was sure they must be frightful places. All desire for icecream was lost in a wave of nausea, but I was far too overawed by this big man to express my anxiety – even when he lifted me over the granite wall and the eerie darkness of the trees engulfed us. Not even the birds were singing.

Forest paths all look much the same, and we had walked until my strength had almost gone before he admitted we were lost.

'Never mind,' he said, 'I'm sure we just need to keep going downhill and we'll hit the sea eventually.' So we left the comparative safety of the track, and plunged in among the trees themselves – where, of course, the wolves and trolls were sure to live!

Branches scratched my face and pulled my hair, slippery roots tripped me up, and huge wood ants' nests impeded my progress. Yet the pain from my grazed knees and scratches was nothing in comparison to my terror of those wolves. I did not actually see one, but I was sure their yellow eyes were looking at me from the black holes between the rocks and moss-covered boulders.

It was like the worst nightmare I ever had, but suddenly everything changed. A huge hand came down from high above me and took mine. It was warm and reassuring, and so big that it engulfed my wrist and forearm as well as my hand.

'Come on, you're doing well, I'm proud of you,' said my father. 'We'll remember this adventure all our lives.' Somehow, it was easy after that. His hand held me up; when I slipped, it stopped me from falling – lifting me right over those painful boulders and piles of sharp pine needles. We began to talk, even laugh, as we struggled along together, brought close by shared adversity.

When we finally discovered a stile leading into a field, we both whooped with joy because we saw the village below us with the sea beyond. 'Come on,' he said, 'let's run so we can get there before they

---

*You can sleep without fear; you need not be afraid of disaster . . . for the Lord is with you; he protects you.* (Prov. 3:24–26, LB)

close the shop.' Icecream never tasted so good, and we drove back triumphantly in a taxi.

That walk through the forest holding hands established a relationship of love and trust with my father that lasted for the rest of his life. 'My soul clings to you; your right hand upholds me,' says Psalm 63:8 (NIV). Since then, I have often thought that the art of clinging to God's hand is easiest to learn during the times of greatest fear. As Psalm 37:23 (NIV) adds, 'If the Lord delights in a man's way, he makes his steps firm; though he stumble, he will not fall, for the Lord upholds him with his hand.'

## The 'Hold Up' Factor

Five years ago, Joyce had a breast lump removed. It was benign and no further treatment was necessary, yet she has never recovered. She looks ill, always seems to be in pain, and suffers from all kinds of unpleasant symptoms. She has had to give up her job as a nursing sister and spends most of her time in bed. Yet endless visits to many different hospitals and all kinds of tests and investigations have never shown anything wrong physically. She is not unique in her suffering. Recent studies carried out by Manchester University's Department of Psychiatry and the Institute of Psychiatry in London have confirmed that nearly a third of all patients who go to their GPs with a physical symptom have no detectable physical illness.

Just a few days after Joyce had her operation to remove the lump, her husband died, and three months later their only son went off to university. Was it the fear of life on her own and the demands of a stressful job that trapped Joyce permanently in her 'broken teapot'? Could illness have become her way out of situations she felt too afraid to face?

> *Don't worry about anything; instead, pray about everything; tell God your needs and don't forget to thank him for his answers. If you do this you will experience God's peace, which is far more wonderful than the human mind can understand. His peace will keep your thoughts and your hearts quiet and at rest as you trust in Christ Jesus.* (Phil. 4:6–7, LB)

No one can answer that question, but many doctors have always maintained that how we think and feel influences our physical health enormously. We are not only bodies; we are minds and spirits as well. One man can have a serious heart attack, but be back playing golf again a few months later, while another man suffering an attack of similar severity is so afraid of further trouble that he wraps himself in cottonwool and stays an invalid for the rest of his life.

The doctor in charge of the largest Intensive Care Unit in the USA was recently interviewed on television. He said his research showed that fear plays an important part in a patient's rate of recovery. When patients who are fearful and apprehensive are admitted for major surgery, they are likely to take longer to recover, require higher doses of analgesics and face a greater chance of post-operative complications than patients who are not afraid.

I bumped into Joyce the other day, hobbling painfully into the post office with the help of a stick. 'It's my hip,' she complained, 'but the doctor says there's nothing he can do. I reckon he thinks I'm making it up,' she added with a sigh. The bleak expression on her face has haunted me ever since.

Dr David Goldberg, Professor of Psychiatry at Withington Hospital in Manchester, maintains that although many doctors dismiss psychosomatic pain as imaginary and incurable, the pain experienced can be greater than that suffered by patients with organic disease. Yet they receive little sympathy from the rest of the world. People like Joyce are written off as hypochondriacs and malingerers, but they *are* ill – ill with fear. They are the truly 'incurable', because no modern drugs or miracle surgery can give them back their health.*

There is hope, however, even for these 'no-hopers'. Jesus can mend the unmendable. I believe that he is saying to all those who cannot face getting back into 'real' life again and feel they may be retreating into illness: 'Will you trust me – even in the grip of such a huge fear? I am not asking you to travel alone along the road that lies ahead; I will

* Obviously not all psychosomatic illness is caused by fear.

---

*There is something supernatural in all disease which man cannot explain.* (Hippocrates, the pioneer of the science of medicine)

walk it with you. Let me flood your mind, soul and body with my own health and vitality. I came to give you life in all its abundance – will you say "yes" to that life and walk into it with me?'

> See! The winter is past;
> the rains are over and gone.
> Flowers appear on the earth;
> the season of singing has come,
> the cooing of doves is heard in our land.

> The fig-tree forms its early fruit;
> the blossoming vines spread their fragrance.
> Arise, come, my darling; my beautiful one,
> come with me.
> (Song of Songs 2:11–13, NIV)

### Practical Tips for Coping with Fear

#### *Talk about it*

Talking out our fears usually helps a great deal. The smaller worries are easy: most of us discuss those so easily that the rest of the world runs for cover when they see us coming! It is the really enormous fears that we find hard to put into words, yet by doing so we can diminish them in size quite dramatically.

Dick had been in hospital for three weeks, undergoing extensive surgery. He never asked the medical staff about their diagnosis, and he avoided the subject when his family and friends visited him. He was pretty sure he knew what was wrong, but somehow he simply could not put his worst fears into words. At night, when the ward was quiet at last, he would lie longing for sleep, but it was then that these nameless, unexpressed fears loomed very large, and his whole body felt so rigid and stiff that sleep was quite impossible.

---

*Save me from sinking in the mud; keep me safe from my enemies, safe from the deep water. Don't let the flood come over me; don't let me drown in the depths or sink into the grave.* (Ps. 69:14–15, GNB)

---

One morning, another patient stopped by his bed for a chat. 'You've got cancer too, haven't you?' he said casually. 'I know because I've just had the same op., and I heard the doctors talking about you.'

One hour later they were still talking, and later that afternoon, when Dick's wife came to see him she said, 'What's happened to you? You look ever so much better. Have they changed your drugs or something?' Dick smiled. He knew it was talking that had helped him, not pills, and that night he slept wonderfully.

A week later, when he left hospital, he soon discovered that it is one thing to talk to another patient, but quite another to discuss your fears with a wife and family. As the weeks went by, a prickly silence settled over the household. 'How much have they been told?' Dick wondered, while his family thought, 'He doesn't seem to have a clue what's wrong.' In the end, the atmosphere became so tense and relationships so strained that a wise Macmillan nurse gently but firmly helped Dick and his wife to share their feelings with one another. The relief was enormous.

'I was waiting for you to say something,' said Dick.

'And I was waiting for *you* to say something,' said his wife. The shadow that had begun to divide them melted away, and they were close to each other again.

### A more energetic method

Martin Luther was often full of fear, and this was his coping strategy: 'When I am assailed with heavy tribulation, I rush out among my pigs, rather than remain alone.' On another occasion he said, 'I exorcise the devil when I harness the horse and spread manure upon my fields.'

My friend Ruth devised a rather less smelly way of coping. She found the first few months after her husband died very difficult indeed.

> *Do not be afraid – I will save you. I have called you by name – you are mine. When you pass through deep waters, I will be with you; your troubles will not overwhelm you. When you pass through fire you will not be burnt; the hard trials that come will not hurt you. (Isa. 43:1–2, GNB)*

'I've always been an early bird,' she told me. 'I go downstairs, make a pot of tea, and just sit with the Lord for an hour before breakfast. For years that's been my best time of the day, but after Brian died I found all the worries came crowding in on me as I sat there in the mornings. I struggled with them, told myself off, and generally felt wretched. Then I decided to try a change of routine. I still got up early, but, instead of my "quiet time", I got the hoover out and tackled the cleaning. Did my bits of cooking for the day, scrubbed the kitchen floor, scoured the bath – anything I could think of that was downright physical. Then at eight o'clock I was good and tired. I seemed to have used up all that nervous energy, and I was ready to sit down with the Lord quietly.'

### The irritating method

There is nothing so maddening as being told to 'count your blessings', but that was exactly what helped George, a businessman with a very stressful workload. 'Probably most people get things completely out of proportion if they wake in the night,' he said, 'and their worries seem to spin round and round like a whirlpool. That's just how I felt all day long as well, when I got into that anxiety state a few years back. I just couldn't seem to control my thoughts at all – until I decided to be positive, and made myself concentrate on what was going right, rather than always thinking about the things that were going wrong.'

### Walking away

People who are born with naturally placid temperaments can often look down on us born worriers and condemn us as unspiritual. Yet if we can use worry as a trigger for prayer, then surely the more we worry the better! At least, that was always my theory until one day I realised that expressing my worries to God in prayer was not at all the same thing as *relinquishing* them to him in faith.

When our oldest daughter Sarah left home and went to university, she was the first of our six 'chicks' to leave the nest. I knew that her faith had been very wobbly during her 'A' level years, and she made no secret of the fact that she wanted to 'experience Oxford' in the fullest sense of the word and not be tied down by some 'stuffy old Christian Union'. She had every intention of leaving God behind at home. I can't ever remember being more worried than I was the first few days after she had gone. I knew the people she met during her freshers' week and the societies she joined could influence the rest of her life. For eighteen years I had always been able to take care of her in thousands of ways; now she was right out of my control and influence. 'Turn your worries into prayer,' I reminded myself firmly. So I sent a constant barrage of muttered prayers aloft day and night.

'Oh Lord, help her. Oh Lord, be with her. Oh Lord, help her . . .' On and on it went like a chant, but I was so preoccupied that I burnt the toast, blackened the sausages, forgot messages, and generally rendered myself useless with worry.

'This can't go on,' I told myself after a few days. 'I'm not really praying because there's no trust involved.'

So I went up to Sarah's unnaturally tidy bedroom and on a shelf I found my mother's old Bible, worn and shabby with many years of use. I opened it and laid it down on Sarah's bed. Then I wrote her name on a scrap of paper and laid it on the Bible.

'Lord,' I said, 'here she is. She is *yours*.'

Then I closed the Bible, enclosing the piece of paper – 'Just like the hands of God,' I thought, as I turned and deliberately went away, leaving her in his care. Each morning I went back, opened the Bible, and prayed again for Sarah in detail, but finally I would close the Bible and relinquish my concern by the simple act of walking away. For me, prayer can be a bit abstract and intangible sometimes, so doing something active like that helps me a lot.

A few days after I had started to pray like that, we had a phone call from the John Radcliffe Hospital in Oxford. A voice said, 'Sarah has been involved in an accident, and she has back injuries.'

'Fine way you have of looking after her,' was my unworthy prayer as we drove down the motorway. Sarah spent the rest of that term on her back, isolated from all her new friends and involvements.

'When I came up to Oxford,' she told me later, 'I thought I didn't need God any more, but as I lay in hospital I knew that I did.' She gave herself to him in a new, adult way, and was able to lead many other people to him during her university years. God really did know what he was doing.

## A Meditation

It was the last time they would all be together like this. None of them realised that, of course, except perhaps Judas. The shadow of a terrible sin already darkened his face as he sat there, fiddling nervously with a piece of bread. Poor Judas, there was still time to change his mind, but when he finally got up and sidled away into the darkness, the sorrow he left behind in the heart of Jesus must have been terrible.

However, there were still the other eleven, and Jesus needed to turn his attention to them, because time was running out and he had so many important things to say. They had been with him constantly, working, travelling, eating, laughing and facing all kinds of adventures together. And here they all were at the end of those three special years, enjoying a meal that they had no idea would seem so significant in the years ahead. He loved them so much as he looked round at their happy faces, laughing in the candlelight.

'My children, I shall not be with you very much longer,' he said gently. Like anyone else who saw death approaching, he wanted to give these people he loved the precious assets he had valued most in life – just as silver spoons, four-poster beds and stately homes have been handed safely on through the years. He had no money to leave them, not even a little carpenter's business, and his clothes were shabby from the dusty roads, but he had something far more valuable than anything else. What good are silver spoons, fine furniture or grand houses if their owner is tormented by fear? Or money, work and clothes to someone who is too miserable to enjoy them? So looking round he said to them:

'Peace is what I leave with you; it is my own peace that I give you . . . Do not be worried and upset; do not be afraid' (John 14:27, GNB); 'I have told you this so that my joy may be in you and that your joy may be complete' (John 15:11, GNB). Peace and joy are the perfect antidotes to fear and misery.

His heart must have been heavy as he thought how much they would need their inheritance in the years to come. He knew they must face the terror of persecution, the fear of travelling to dangerous places, storms at sea, shipwrecks, aching homesickness, hunger, cruel beatings, stonings, insults and lying accusations, then the lonely dungeons and, for most of them, a violent, painful death.

Yes, he knew they would often be afraid, and how he must have longed to save them from it all. He had the power to do so; he could have changed them all into angelic beings who were above human cruelty, but he needed them to be men for a little while longer. The job of telling the rest of us about his love could only be done by human beings. So he gave them his peace to keep their hearts and minds through the tensions and anxieties, and his own personal brand of joy to give them strength to face everything that mankind, and even Satan himself, would throw at them. Those eleven men have handed that inheritance on down through the generations, so that this 'peacejoy' can be ours too – just for the asking.

## A Prayer

*'Come to me all you who are tired of being afraid . . . "For I, the Lord your God, hold your right hand; I, Who say to you, Fear not, I will help you".'* (Isa. 41:13, AMP)

Lord, I have that one great dread – you know the one I mean – my worst fear. To me it feels like my own Calvary, and the path towards it resembles a crucifixion. I know that thinking about it is probably worse than the actual reality will be when it comes, but you too were afraid in your Gethsemane. You cried out to your father God, pleading with him to change his mind and take the horrible cup away from you. You were a man, and you were afraid like the rest of us. Yet you took your fears and walked with them right to the bitter end. You faced that worst fear of all, the cross itself, and you walked right through it to the far side, and beyond to resurrection and renewal.

Lord, help me to do the same. I want to avoid my Calvary just as you did, but I know there is only one way – and that is to go forward towards it and then through it to the far side. But I am still afraid, I am not as brave as you. But I give you my fear, and I ask for your help as you walk beside me towards the thing I dread. 'Even if I go through the deepest darkness, I will not be afraid, Lord, for you are with me . . . I know that your goodness and love will be with me all my life' (Ps. 23:4, 6, GNB).

## STOP FOR A MOMENT

*It was in Ireland that I discovered something that has helped me profoundly in coping with just about every single emotion connected with the Broken Teapot Syndrome. One glorious sunny afternoon a friend took us for a drive along a rocky Irish coast road. The sea was actually turquoise as it lapped round the little coves and sandy bays, and tall stone towers stood at intervals along the cliffs.*

*'Why don't the lighthouses have any doors?' we asked.*

*'Because they're Irish,' our friend replied with a twinkle in his eyes. 'Hundreds of years ago, all along these shores, were little sleepy fishing villages full of happy people minding their own business, when along came the Vikings in their long boats. Up the beach they came and terror reigned. Every man killed, the women raped, and the children taken as slaves. Crops and huts burnt to the ground, and nothing left to show for it but corpses.' He was warming to his story even if it was growing a little in the telling. 'Well, we Irish didn't like that, so we decided to build these high towers. A wee man would be sitting at the top, looking out to sea. When the raiders were sighted, he rang a bell so everyone could run for safety into the tower.'*

*'But how did they get in without a door?' I protested.*

*'The door was high up on the side of the tower, and the wee man would let down a rope ladder. When the last man was inside, he'd pull it back up again. Then there'd be nothing at all the old Vikings could do but go home again.'*

*'Didn't they wait until the people were hungry enough to come out?' I suggested.*

*'Sure, but the tower would be filled with all the provisions they could ever need. So, because those towers were there, the people could live happily, knowing there was always somewhere safe where they could run.'*

*Later I had to speak in a church and the first song they sang was based on Proverbs 18:10 (NIV): 'The name of the Lord is a strong tower; the righteous run to it and are safe.' The verse meant everything to me after seeing those strong towers of refuge earlier in the day. I realised that words like 'fortress', 'stronghold' and 'refuge' are often used to describe the Lord in the Old Testament, and of course Paul loves telling us about all the benefits we receive when we are 'in Christ'.*

*The concept of the Lord being like a huge, safe, protective fortress to which I can run and be safe whenever the need arises has been such a* help ever since. One day, for instance, I was furiously angry. Someone close to me was making my life extremely difficult without any apparent concern or regret. For months I had struggled with my feelings until irritation had become outrage, and on this particular day I felt my anger getting quite out of control. So I took my dog Brodie to a lonely place in the countryside and stamped round the fields muttering, growling and even shouting when I was quite sure no one was within earshot.

'Lord, take this anger away!' I kept demanding as I shook my fist heavenwards. But he did nothing to help me at all, and if anything my rage became even more intense. Then suddenly I remembered those Irish towers, but how did you get into a tower if it was not made of solid stone? Suddenly, it dawned on me: it was the name of the Lord that was the strong tower. Out loud I began to say the name of Jesus, and round and round the muddy field I stamped, repeating it all the while. At first, nothing happened, and I felt such a fool; but there is an enormous, earth-shaking, life-changing power in the actual name of Jesus Christ. Before long, I began to feel the anger recede, and a tangible calm like strong walls began to rise up around me. I was safely 'inside the strong tower' by the time Brodie and I finally reached home, wet and mud splattered, and my anger over that particular situation has never troubled me since.

The following week I told someone else about this coping strategy when she told me about her fear of crowded places. She looked most doubtful when I explained the idea to her, but later that day she phoned to say, 'It worked! As soon as I began to say the name of Jesus I felt as if safe walls were rising up all around me, my heart beat slowed down, and my breathing returned to normal.'

You probably won't believe that this works until you try it. So why not decide now that the next time you are overrun by your particular 'Viking', you will run into Jesus himself by repeating his name. Like the Irish towers that contained all the necessary provisions, when we are 'in Christ' we really can find the antidote to whatever negative emotion is attacking us at the time. 'In Christ' you have 'every spiritual blessing' (Eph. 1:3, NIV) and 'everything we need for life and godliness' (2 Pet. 1:3, NIV).

# 6

# DESPAIR AND DEPRESSION

Sadness and sorrow are understandable after the loss of something or someone very precious, but many Christians seem to feel that despair and depression are right out of bounds! Yet experts say that practically all human beings go through some degree of depression within the first five years after a major loss. Doctors describe it as reactive depression. For some it is no more than feeling 'a bit low' for a few weeks, while others may spend a year or more feeling that life is grey and pointless and not worth the effort. In its most acute form, it can cause a total failure to function normally, 'a complete break-down', and rest, medication and even hospitalisation are necessary. In all its forms, reactive depression is normal – even for Christians; yet so many look on with disapproval when one of the others slithers down the 'black snake' and lands on the darkest square on the game board.

Depression *is* the very roughest part of the entire Broken Teapot Syndrome. I remember feeling utterly desolate. A misty, grey cloud shrouded me constantly, affecting my every action, thought and feeling. Worst of all, God seemed to have abandoned me, just when I needed him most.

These days I am quite often asked to be part of seminars for Christians going through depression – or living with someone who is – and I asked one group recently to write down in a few words how they felt. Here are some of their responses:

*Surely there is no greater attachment in life than the attachment to your self-image?* (Michael Hanson)

'I can't feel that God's there any more.'
'God seems to be hiding his face from me.'
'God is out of sight and between us is a blank, black wall.'
'I've lost touch with God and my Christian life's gone dead.'
'Darkness with no light at the end of the tunnel.'
'No point in going on, there's nothing to live for.'
'Like being in a deep dark well.'
'Everything's grey. The world's lost all colour.'
'As I wake up I feel as if a load of heavy, wet sand is pouring over me, pushing me down into the bed. Can't face the day. Can't make decisions – not even what to wear.'
'A black cloud hiding the sun and covering the horizon.'

King David wrote: 'Lord, I call to you for help; every morning I pray to you. Why do you reject me, Lord? Why do you turn away from me?' (Ps. 88:13–14, GNB.) And in Proverbs it says: 'A man's spirit sustains him in sickness, but a crushed spirit who can bear?' (Prov. 18:14, NIV.)

## Doubts

Doubts about God's love, and even his existence, also seem to come with the 'depression package' and many people in the seminars confessed they were plagued by them:

'I can't believe God loves me – because I'm so totally worthless myself, I assume he thinks the same.'
'I sometimes think he must be a sadist to let me go through something like this.'
In Lamentations it says: 'I am one who knows what it is to be punished by God. He drove me deeper and deeper into darkness and beat me again and again with merciless blows' (Lam. 3:1–3, GNB).
It is possible to be depressed without feeling gloomy and doleful at

---

*Answer me now, Lord! I have lost all hope. Don't hide yourself from me . . . Remind me each morning of your constant love, for I put my trust in you.* (Ps. 143:7–8, GNB)

all, and these doubts may be the only symptom that shows. So instead of seeing these doubts as part of the depression and accepting that they will pass in time, we begin to feel we are losing our faith and failing completely.

## Hopelessness

It is useless to talk brightly about the 'process of change' to people who are depressed, or to remind them that God is moving them on into a new kind of life. Depression takes away all hope for the future and makes life today feel pointless and futile. Verses like 'Surely goodness and mercy shall follow me all the days of my life' (Ps. 23:6, AV) are hard to believe when you are convinced that this state of despair is going to be permanent. 'I'm never going to get out of this,' commented one member of the seminar group.

King Solomon described his feelings like this: 'It is useless, useless, said the Philosopher. Life is useless, all useless. You spend your life working, labouring, and what do you have to show for it?' (Eccles. 1:2–3, GNB.)

## Tiredness and Lethargy

Depression is not only a feeling of despair, but an illness that affects the emotions, the body and the mind. Many physical symptoms seem to be part of it, and these often take people by surprise:

'I feel tired and lethargic all the time.'
'All motivation has gone.'
'The day stretches ahead endlessly. I'm bored, but there's no energy to do anything interesting.'
'My house is a tip, but I can't be bothered.'

Comments from 'the spectators', such as 'Why don't you just pull yourself together and snap out of it?', can hurt terribly, because you

*The Lord is close to the broken-hearted and saves those who are crushed in spirit.* (Ps. 34:18, NIV)

*would* – if only you *could*! Such people force you to look on the bright side when, from where you stand, there is no bright side to see.

## Christians and Depression

Perhaps it is the fear of that kind of misunderstanding that makes many of us keep quiet about how we are really feeling. To me, depression felt like utter failure. 'As a Christian, I shouldn't feel like this' is something people often say in the seminars. Perhaps many of us have a mental image of the 'Christian' we feel we ought to be, someone who is constantly full of joy, and who dashes round helping people who are miserable.

I now realise that our friend George thought he should be like that. He was part of a whole gang of friends that Tony and I used to go around with before we were married. None of us ever realised that George was depressed after his particular 'teapot' broke, so we were badly shaken when we heard that he had hanged himself. He left a note telling us he was sorry, but he could no longer live with the hypocrisy of knowing he ought to be able to praise God when he no longer felt that he could.

George died more than twenty-five years ago, but his memory still haunts me. If only we had realised he was feeling so bad, and if only he had gone to his doctor for help. It is because of George that I always urge people who admit they are depressed to swallow their pride and go and see their GP. Dr Marion Ashton, a psychiatrist, once told me that, in her opinion, Christians were the most difficult group of patients to treat.* 'They find it so hard to admit they are depressed, so they may function below their potential for years, feeling tired and lacking enthusiasm. Medical science could do so much to help them, if only they could be brave enough to go to their doctor and receive his treatment as a gift from God.'

Perhaps another reason for the stigma attached to being depressed

* See *Where Have You Gone God?*

O my soul, why be so gloomy and discouraged? Trust in God! . . . he will make me smile again, for he is my God! (Ps. 43:5, LB)

is that it can be caused by some deepseated spiritual problems. I remember once, when I was depressed, listening to a tape on the subject by a leading Christian conference speaker. While I lay in my bed cringing, he reeled off a long list of things that can cause depression:

- unresolved conflicts
- blocked goals
- swallowed anger
- unconfessed sin
- bitterness
- lack of forgiveness
- self-pity
- delayed or long-denied grief
- unacknowledged guilt

There were probably more things that I have forgotten, but I do remember trying to work out which ones were behind all my misery. In the end I became so upset that I felt they probably *all* were, and I wanted to sink through the bed in shame. What if my friends at church discovered what a disgrace I was as a Christian? I was sure they would all be running down the checklist with me in mind if they ever guessed I was depressed. I never actually told anyone, not even my husband or my two best friends. Perhaps it was easier for me to deceive everyone because I was physically ill at the time, and that created a perfect smokescreen – as it does for many people.

Of course, all those things listed above can cause depression, but during the Broken Teapot Syndrome the most usual cause is a reaction to the trauma we have recently gone through. Therefore it is probably wiser, while we are depressed, not to go digging down looking for reasons when all our energy is needed just to survive through the next hour.

---

*Praise be to . . . the God of all comfort, who comforts us in all our troubles, so that we can comfort those in any trouble with the comfort we ourselves have received from God.* (2 Cor. 1:3,4, NIV)

## Does Anything Help?

Looking back at my own depression and by talking to many other sufferers, I have managed to glean just a few suggestions that do seem to help some people, some of the time.

### *It will pass*

Repeating the three words 'it will pass' has been a real help to several people – simply because they are true. This depression *will* go away eventually, even though we may find that hard to believe at the time.

### *Go with the flow*

That is another good little phrase to remember. Fighting depression and allowing yourself to become agitated or angry about it only seems to make things worse. Looking for instant escape routes or sudden healing can lead to disappointment and further despair. Although there are people who have been healed instantly through prayer, depression seems to lift very gradually for most of us – so usually it is best just to keep plodding on through to the other side.

### *Look out for surprises*

I have a battered old notebook that I call my prayer journal, and in it I found these words that I wrote because I felt they were from God:

'Look carefully as you walk through today. I made so many beautiful things, which others say are useless. Savour them with me. Relish these small surprises.

'The sun shafting through a chink in the curtains and making all that dust which irritates you dance and swirl in a world of exquisite colour.

'Or the intricate pattern on the wings of the fly that buzzes against the glass at your window – and nearly drives you mad. The tiny

---

*Don't you think that some of us must know the trials of misty weather if we are to be enabled to understand when others are in the mists?* (Amy Carmichael)

bubbles reflecting the light in yesterday's glass of stale water standing forgotten on the table.

'Out of these tiny glimmers of hope your joy will be reborn. I have placed these surprises ready for you to discover along the path today, so watch out for them carefully because they could easily be missed.'

I can remember deliberately looking out each day for one of these unusual 'treasures of darkness' (Isa. 45:3, NIV), and then noting it down in my diary at night.

Open our eyes, thou sun of life and gladness,
That we may see that glorious world of thine!
It shines for us in vain,
While drooping sadness enfolds us here like mist. (Keble)

### Act as if

Blaise Pascal, the seventeenth-century mathematician and theologian, once said that if our faith has gone, we need to act as if we still possessed it until it returns. Those three words, 'act as if', have not only been a help to me over the doubts, but in all kinds of other situations as well.

A friend of mine who is part of an amateur dramatic society had to play the part of a very depressed woman in a play that they performed seven nights in a row. She was excellent in the part, but by the Friday she admitted she had let herself get into it a bit too well! 'I began to feel depressed myself. I couldn't switch it off somehow. I found myself shuffling about with my shoulders drooping or flopping wearily into a chair with a heavy sigh. When I heard myself talking in a minor key with all my sentences going downhill at the end, I thought, "I'll be glad when Saturday night's over!"'

If 'acting depressed' can make you feel depressed, then might it not work the other way round? It has been medically proved that a smile on the outside can actually make you feel better on the inside – but if

---

*I am weak and poor, O Lord, but you have not forgotten me. You are my Saviour and my God – hurry to my aid! (Ps. 40:17, GNB.) I am poor and needy, but the Lord takes thought and plans for me. (Ps. 40:17)*

anyone had suggested that I try that when I was depressed, I might well have hit them!

### God still believes in you

When I felt my faith in God's love was slipping away, I used to panic because I thought that if I lost it completely he would not be able to help me any more. Thinking like that is just about as stupid as the small child who feels invisible when he closes his eyes! Francis James put it like this: 'It is not my grasp of God that matters most, but His grasp of me. The thing that matters most is not even my consciousness that He holds me fast, but just the blessed fact of it.'

### 'It is not your faith that counts, but God's faithfulness'

Once, after weeks of trying to work up faith for healing, our vicar said something that helped me profoundly. 'It's not our faith that counts, but God's faithfulness.' The relief was enormous, particularly when he added, 'We do not need to have a great faith, we just have to trust a great Saviour.'

### Find a prayer partner

I would not tell anyone I was depressed, so no one was specifically praying for my protection in the wilderness. When I finally dared tell the hospital chaplain,* he began to pray for me every day; it was then that my depression began to lift.

We should never underestimate prayer. It connects us to the limitless power of God, just as an electrical plug pushed into the socket puts all the gigantic power of electricity at our disposal. I don't understand *why* prayer works, any more than I understand electricity. I just know they both do work! Find someone who will pray for you regularly – although not necessarily *with* you, because that

---

\* See *Unexpected Healing*, p. 75.

---

> The Lord's unfailing love and mercy still continue, fresh as the morning, as sure as the sunrise. The Lord is all I have, and so I put my hope in him. (Lam. 3:22–24, GNB)

might become the kind of strain you cannot take when you are depressed.

### Tell God how you feel

I found it very hard to tell God how I felt, because prayer was impossible at first. The only way I could communicate with God was by writing him short notes in my journal. Looking back at them now, I am horrified at how rude some of them were, but at the time it really helped me to be brutally honest. Later, when I finally confided in the chaplain, he reassured me greatly by pointing out that Jesus had also been honest like that when he expressed his anguish without any reserve whatsoever. As he hung alone in the darkness on the cross, he felt (as I was also feeling) that his Father had abandoned him completely. So he summoned up his last scrap of strength and cried out into the lonely darkness, 'My God, My God, why have you abandoned me?' Just knowing he understood from experience how I was feeling was a vast comfort at the time.

### An alternative way of communicating

Even writing notes to God was quite beyond my friend Ruth after she had spent eighteen months nursing her husband through cancer:

'When he was gone, praying or going to church were "out" for at least six months. I felt brain dead, and the hymns unhinged me completely. So I used to creep into church during the week sometimes when no one was there, and sit quietly in a pew. Just being with God. Not saying anything, just reminding myself that he could see just how I felt. I always felt comforted as I walked back home.'

### Beware of the Blankets and Sheets

May, who lives alone, was signed off work for three months last year

---

*All your waves and billows have gone over me, and floods of sorrow pour upon me like a thundering cataract. Yet day by day the Lord also pours out his steadfast love upon me. (Ps 42:7–8, LB)*

with depression. 'I would wake up in the morning feeling so terrible that I couldn't face the day, so I often used to pull the bedclothes over my head and just stay there. Yet when I did make the effort to get up, even if dressing, washing and doing my hair exhausted me completely, I felt so much better for doing it. I only sat in the chair all day, but at least I felt more like a human being. Perhaps when you don't feel good, you can try and look good!'

Jenny found it helped if she made herself go out of her house, even if it was only to the shop on the corner. By the time she had chatted to someone about the weather and the price of butter, she felt more in touch with ordinary, everyday life.

## Beware of Amateur Psychiatrists

As we have seen in other stages of the Broken Teapot Syndrome, talking about how we feel is vital – but never more so than during depression. However, talking to the wrong people can be disastrous. There are far too many well-meaning people these days who see themselves as amateur psychiatrists. If we begin to open ourselves up to them they can go crashing around our subconscious minds in hobnail boots, or compound our sense of worthlessness by their condemnation. One nineteen-year-old girl who was being 'counselled' by someone like that was told to throw away all the drugs the doctor had prescribed because she was 'now healed'. However, she did not *feel* healed, and a week later she jumped in front of a train.

There are certain people who are experienced and recognised counsellors and, although they have received a training, they work under the control and guidance of the Holy Spirit. Secular counsellors and psychologists can help us to understand our hurts, but Jesus can actually heal them; and he seems to do this most often through the prayers of his servants. You are not alone: there is a whole network of people who want to allow the compassion of Jesus to flow through their personalities to help you. It is better to talk to an experienced counsellor than a hundred of the other kind.

---

*Let he who judges me, first walk two weeks in my moccasins.* (Red Indian proverb)

---

## Beware of the 'Hold Up' Factor

When we are severely depressed we carry such a vast burden of misery that we cannot add to it by considering the problems or needs of anyone else. *We* become the centre of our own universe, and see others only as they relate to us – what they do for us and give to us. Their problems, feelings or needs cease to exist, and we cannot reach out to them in order to give them any help or emotional support. We resemble the following diagram: looking to others to meet our needs, but unable to do anything in return.

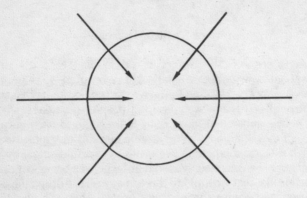

The opposite diagram represents a person before depression: receiving help and support, but able to give to others in return.

During the worst of the depression we cannot help but resemble the first diagram. As the depression lifts, however, the self-absorption can remain and become a way of life. Negative attitudes and self-centred thought patterns can be acquired during depression, and self-pity makes us feel everyone else must be better off than we are. Some people stay trapped like this permanently, so absorbed by their own needs and problems that they lose the habit of noticing that other people have pressures too. People trapped like this talk about themselves all the time, and demand so much from others that they drain them dry.

---

*This land that was desolate is become like the garden of Eden.* (Ezek. 36:35, AV)

---

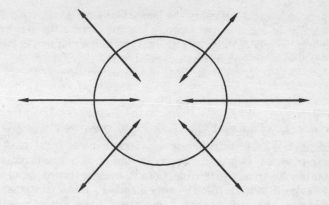

*Turning the arrows back outwards again*

My depression was definitely on the way out when it dawned on me that I was in danger of being trapped by this particular 'hold up' factor. I wrote one of my notes to God in my diary that day: 'This book is full of endless prayers for me, but I never seem to pray for other people any more, do I?' The realisation came because I had looked at Tony. It sounds odd, living with someone and *not* looking at them, but that day I had noticed how worn and tired his face looked, and I remember thinking, 'This depression has been horrible for me, but I bet it's been even worse for Tony.'

Sometime during the following week, my friend Grace rang to say she was coming to see me. She is the most sympathetic and sensitive friend I have ever had, and it is always easy (and safe) to pour out all my worries to her; but that day I made a conscious decision that I would also ask her how *she* was feeling, and then really listen when she told me.

The next step was to ring someone who I knew was feeling low as

> *Some wandered in the trackless desert and could not find their way to a city to live in. They were hungry and thirsty and had given up all hope. Then in their trouble they called to the Lord, and he saved them from their distress. He led them by a straight road to a city where they could live. (Ps. 107:4–7, GNB)*

well. Sounds easy! But using the phone had terrified me for months. Gradually, in small ways, we have to start turning the arrows and pointing them back outwards again. I found it a real battle, but it is the only way to combat this destructive 'hold up' factor.

## The Challenge

All this could make some people say, 'But I've lost my self-confidence. I can't help being self-centred, now that I can't face meeting people.' Depression certainly robs us of our self-confidence, but is that loss really so terrible? Could it even be turned round to our advantage if it were placed in the hands of Jesus? Perhaps 'self'-confidence is not so important as most people nowadays think that it is. Maybe 'God'-confidence is what we need even more.

Surely in this stage God is asking:

- 'Will you allow me to come into the centre of your self-absorption? Will you let me fill the "self" part of you – the self-occupied, self-fulfilled, self-assertive, self-conscious place at the core of your being?'
- 'Will you let me be your confidence, in place of the self-confidence you have lost? Then together we can go out to other people – and you will be able to see them as I see them, and I will be able to meet their needs through you.'

'Blessed is the man who trusts in the Lord whose confidence is in him' (Jer. 17: 7, NIV).

One summer afternoon in 1989 I was sitting in my wheelchair overlooking the beach on which my children were playing. For some months I had been slightly depressed, and I had so hoped this holiday in Devon would see the end of it. By that time I had been ill for seven years, and the strain of coping with the pain and weakness on top of trying to be a good mum, write books and speak at

---

*He changed deserts into pools of water and dry land into flowing springs. He let hungry people settle there, and they built a city to live in. They sowed the fields and planted grapevines and reaped an abundant harvest.* (Ps. 107:35–37, GNB)

meetings was all proving a bit too much. (Those were the days when I was still trying to prove that I was not inadequate.)

As I sat there, I hated the thought of going home the next day and having to get back into 'life' again. The depression had certainly broken the small amount of self-confidence I had regained since I first became ill. I couldn't face the half-finished book that lurked in my computer and the speaking engagements that glared at me from my diary. I didn't pray; I just sat there gazing bleakly at the tide slapping and sucking round a red Devon rock just beyond the beach. Suddenly, I knew that Jesus himself was standing on that rock. I did not actually see him, but I knew he was there, and the sense of his presence was overwhelming. I am embarrassed to say that I did not dissolve into a flood of praise – instead, I told him all about my inadequacy and apprehension.

'Why do I always get so scared of doing things and why didn't you make me like all these powerful people who have so many wonderful gifts?' (In other words, 'Why couldn't I have taken after my parents?') Five words instantly popped into my head, and I knew without doubt they were his answer.

'All you need is me.' That puzzled me at first, then gradually I realised he wanted to be everything to me – not only to meet all my needs, but the needs of others through me. I wonder if Paul was describing this when he said, 'I am most happy, then, to be proud of my weaknesses, in order to feel the protection of Christ's power over me . . . For when I am weak, then I am strong' (2 Cor. 12:9–10, GNB).

Ten months later, Jesus healed me physically,* but I have never regained my self-confidence. I am still terrified before I have to stand up to speak or when I begin a writing project, but I am no longer trying desperately to cover up this sense of inadequacy. I see it as an asset, because it makes me turn to the Lord so he can make up for my deficiency.

* See *Unexpected Healing*, Chapter 15.

---

*Who is this coming up from the desert, leaning on her beloved?* (Song of Songs 8:5, LB)

## A Meditation

She stood shaking with fear in the middle of a huge, surging crowd of people. They were pushing and pulling each other – all eager for the best view – but no one ever touched her; they backed away when they recognised who she was. It had been like that ever since the bleeding began twelve years ago, and she had been living with despair ever since. Was it a baby she had lost? A foetus torn prematurely away from the wall of her uterus, leaving a wound that simply refused to heal? The constant bleeding, coupled with her tears of regret, had slowly sapped away her strength, leaving her listless, weary and ill. In her culture, bleeding like that meant she was unclean, and so was anyone that she touched. There could be no more intimacy with her husband – she was not even allowed to cook his food or wash his clothes.

At first they had hoped one of the big city doctors from Jerusalem might be able to help. She had gone from one to the other, using up all her dowry, but their treatments had been humiliating, exhausting and painful. Worst of all, none of them had been successful. Her husband had given up on her – he was within his rights to do so – and now she was alone, her money all gone, and repeated disappointment had gradually killed her hope. She was excluded from her community, the market, the synagogue, and even the temple itself. There was no role for her in life, she was useless, discarded like rubbish, and left to the rot of despair.

Sometimes the emotionally injured feel like that too; their wounds never seem to heal, and over the years they go on bleeding until all their joy has drained away and the perpetual twilight of chronic depression closes around them. Like that woman, they too can go from this person to that in a fruitless search for healing. They expose their souls to painful internal examinations and conflicting diagnoses, until their inner resources of dignity and self-respect have all been absorbed. So often these people are also outcasts in our Christian communities, labelled 'the church problem', and hastily avoided whenever possible.

Jesus was closer now. The clamouring crowd closed in around him, demanding his attention with shrill, excited cries. She had come here to ask for his help as well, yet he was really the last person she wanted to face. This man who said he was the Son of God must surely shrink away from her uncleanness. And all those years of hope deferred had made her wary. Suppose he could not help her either? But there was no one else to turn to now; she was at the end of her endurance and had nothing left to lose.

Standing always made the pain worse, and she was doubled over with it by the time she reached him, almost crawling in the dirt and dust. He had walked on past by the time she managed to reach out towards him and clutch at the hem of his coat.

He stopped. He always stops. If only we would go to him directly instead of putting our hope in all those 'big names' and 'spiritual superstars'. He cannot resist faith that goes to him directly and reaches out a hand in desperation. People who are at the end of themselves can always touch him instantly—as she did. All his undivided attention was hers at that very moment. It can also be ours when we reach out. He may not always help us in the way we expect or as quickly as we would wish, but in his way and in his time he always helps.

He did not draw back disgusted by her as other men would have done. He spoke to her gently, using the most tender and personal name he could have chosen. He called her 'daughter'. Then he sent her away with his own peace resting on her, like a fresh set of clothes or a new identity. No longer just the 'community problem', she was clean. He had taken away her despair, and in exchange he gave her back hope and dignity.

## A Prayer

### For a grey day

*'Come to me all you who are weary from carrying heavy burdens of worthlessness, regret and chronic misery, and I will give you "a crown of beauty instead of ashes, the oil of gladness instead of mourning, and a garment of praise instead of a spirit of despair".'* (Isa. 61:3, NIV)

Lord Jesus, it's an awful place, this wilderness: bleak, empty, desolate. The wind blows dust into my eyes so I can't see where I'm going, and I walk round and round in endless circles, getting nowhere. I'm so tired I just want to stop and crawl away under some rock, but I'm afraid I might be lost for ever if I stop walking. I keep on tripping over jagged little stones on the pathway, and feeling compelled to stoop down and pick them up. These endless stones are my 'if onlys':

- 'If only I . . .'
- 'If only I hadn't . . .'
- 'If only I could still . . .'
- 'If only he was here . . .'
- 'If only I had more . . .'

Collecting these 'if onlys' has become compulsive, and I can't seem to stop. I stuff them into my pockets as I walk, but they are heavy now, there are so many of them. They weigh me down and I'm too tired to carry them any longer.

Can I give all these 'if onlys' to you, Lord? Could I place them into your hands like the little pebbles and shells a child collects and presents to its father for safe keeping? I know that whenever I manage to give you my worthless things, you always give me something far better in exchange. So in the place of all these 'if onlys' and 'might have beens', I will receive from you the new life you said you would give me. The way I feel right now, I find it hard to believe a new life is possible, but I receive it from you by faith – and I thank you.

### For a black day

*'Come to me all you who are torn by anguish and terrible mental distress because I know how it feels . . .'*

*'Then Jesus went to a place called Gethsemane . . . He began to show grief and distress of mind and was deeply depressed. Then he said to them, "My soul is very sad and deeply grieved, so that I am almost dying of sorrow".'* (Matt. 26:36–38, AMP)

*'And being in an agony of mind . . .'* (Luke 22:44, AMP)

*'And he took with Him Peter and James and John, and began to be struck with terror and amazement and deeply troubled and depressed. And He said to them, "My soul is exceedingly sad – overwhelmed with grief so that it almost kills me".'* (Mark 14:33–34, AMP)

Lord, nothing seems to help when I am bound here like this at the very bottom of the deepest pit in the darkest part of the valley I am being forced to struggle through. I can see the faces of my friends peering down at me from high above my head – they are right up there in the sunlight, anxiously watching as I squirm in agony down here below them. *But they can't understand.*

I am glad you are not a God who looks down on me like that, without knowing how it feels. Just remembering that you have been here in this same pit before me is my only shred of comfort at this moment. Yes, that helps so much.

### Perhaps the Lord Might Respond Like This

'You are not alone in that bleak place. I am with you to shield and guard you, even when you cannot feel me near. You think of yourself as useless rubbish, flung away in that wasteland, but to me, who made the entire universe, you are the very apple of my eye; the focus of my attention. I know you find it hard just now to believe that I love you, but I long for you to accept that I do, by faith. I want you to know that I love you now, just as you are this moment. I am not waiting to love you one day when I have rebuilt you and made your life productive and beautiful again. You are the apple of my eye, and there is nothing that you could ever do that would make me love you any more than I do at this moment, because my love for you is complete.'

---

*Even when we are too weak to have any faith left, he remains faithful to us and will help us for he cannot disown us who are part of himself, and he will always carry out his promises to us.* (2 Tim. 2:13 LB)

## STOP FOR A MOMENT

*One of the nastiest things about the Broken Teapot Syndrome is the feeling of being worth nothing in the world and forgotten by other people. 'God can't be interested in me,' we think, 'because I'll never be able to do anything big or important for him.' However, Jesus tells us that this is absolutely not true.*

*That summer when we were in Devon, I felt just like that. It was most frustrating to be in a paradise of cliffs, beaches and lazy blue sea and to have no energy to do more than sit gazing blankly out of the window. Right in front of me was a very high hedge, and among its shiny green leaves lived several billion sparrows – well, it seemed that many to me. I even tried to count them one day, but they acted like sheep and sent me to sleep instantly.*

*As the days slid by, I became increasingly fascinated by those sparrows and the way they repeated the same sequence of activities over and over again throughout each hour of the day. Their routine was always the same:*

*Hop down from the hedge, peck, flutter back up again.*
*Hop down, peck, flutter back up.*
*Hop down, peck, flutter back up.*
*Hop down, peck, . . . flutter back up.*

*And so on, probably thousands of times a day. The sparrows only seemed to take a break when it was time to roost in the hedge for the night.*

*A friend had lent me some sermon tapes for the holiday, and most of them were by a cousin of mine, the Rev. David Pawson. One drowsy, hot afternoon I was listening to one as I watched the inevitable activity in the hedge, then suddenly I heard him mention sparrows: 'Are not two little sparrows sold for a penny? Yet not one of them will fall to the ground without your Father's leave and notice. Even the very hairs of your head are all numbered. Fear not then; you are of more value than many sparrows' (Matt. 10:29–31, AMP).*

*David went on to explain that in biblical times the normal use of the phrase 'fall to the ground' did not mean 'die and fall to the ground', but should really have been translated 'hop to the ground'. He then went on to say, 'It is just conceivable that a loving God might be touched by the tragic death of a poor little sparrow as it keels over and falls off its perch, but that is not what Jesus was saying. He meant that every time each individual sparrow hops to the ground,*

*God knows about it, and is watching with complete attention.'*

*I stopped my cassette player, too amazed to take in anything further.
God Almighty knew each one of those sparrows in the hedge
individually, and watched its 'hop down, peck, flutter back up' routine
every time it ran through it – each and every day of its life. Multiply
that by all the sparrows that 'hop down, peck, flutter back up' in every
corner of the earth and you really begin to see what a staggering thing
Jesus was saying. It occurred to me that Jesus must have enjoyed
watching birds as much as I do, because on another occasion he said,
'Look at the birds of the air . . . your heavenly Father feeds them. Are
you not much more valuable than they?' (Matt. 6:25–26, NIV.) The
value of an object is measured by the price someone is prepared to pay
for it. Two sparrows were only worth one penny, but Jesus thought you
and I so valuable that he was prepared to give up all the riches of
heaven for us.*

# 7

# GUILT

Feelings of guilt, remorse and endless regret play a very large part in the Broken Teapot Syndrome. There are two distinct types of guilt: genuine guilt, when we know for sure that we are to blame for breaking the 'teapot', and false guilt, which is simply a reaction to grief. This counterfeit version traps people on an endless treadmill of self-reproach:

'It's all my fault, if only I'd noticed he wasn't well, and *made* him go to the doctor.'

'I wish I'd gone on that holiday he was always talking about; now it's too late.'

'Perhaps he wouldn't have left me if I'd lost a bit of weight or kept the house a bit tidier.'

'I'm always a failure. Nothing I do ever seems to succeed.'

'Why, oh why, did I lend him the money to buy that motorbike?'

'It must be my fault.'

The last quote is often how parents of handicapped children feel, or patients who receive a grim diagnosis. They seem to feel it is a punishment for some real or imagined failure in the past. People who have been raped or abused may also feel that they were secretly to blame for what happened:

'For three years my eighteen-year-old step-brother used to abuse me sexually,' Penny told me. 'He had a knife, and he said he'd kill me if I didn't go with him to the shed on the allotments and do as he said.

---

*Mere sorrow which sits and weeps out its regrets is not repentance. Repentance is sorrow converted into action.*
(David Augsburger)

I was only eight when it started. Ever since, I've always felt this awful feeling of guilt, like a big black cloud hanging over my head and shoulders. I never dared tell my mum or teacher what was happening because I thought they would say it was my fault, and I suppose that I thought so too, really.

'At church when the word "sinner" was used, I always thought, "that's me". Anything that went wrong in my life, like breaking my leg on holiday or losing my job, I always thought it was only what I deserved. It was years before I dared tell my doctor about the abuse, and when I also told him about my feelings of guilt he just shrugged and said it was perfectly normal – and that people often feel like that after they've been raped or abused.'

The doctor was right: false guilt is normal after trauma, but when we have put God in control of our mending process there must come a time when we climb off this irritating treadmill and ask him to set us free from our misery. He can certainly do this, so long as we are willing to be honest with him. Penny went on struggling with her black cloud of condemnation until, during counselling, she was encouraged to ask God if there was a more valid reason for her feelings of guilt. Almost at once, the word 'hatred' came into her mind.

We are not responsible for what happens to us, but we *are* responsible for our feelings and reactions, i.e. the resentment, self-pity and anger that we feel as a result of the incident. Penny had hated her step-brother, both at the time of the abuse and ever since. She had also implacably refused to forgive him for what he had done to her. Before she could finally be free from the effects of his abuse, she had to repent and let go of her hate. Someone we refuse to forgive is always there, handcuffed to us perpetually, and the only way the chains can be broken is by forgiveness. The difference that this 'liberation' made to Penny's life was enormous, and she found that her false guilt totally disappeared when the genuine guilt that had been hidden beneath it was dealt with at last.

---

*If we say that we have not sinned, we make God out to be a liar, and his word is not in us.* (1 John 1:10, GNB)

### The Red Light on My Washing-machine

During the last thirty years, our permissive society has decided to abolish guilt, declaring it to be old-fashioned and harmful. Yet genuine guilt is a much maligned emotion. On my washing-machine is a red light that flashes when something is going wrong. When I see it, I know I must stop the machine and call in the expert quickly before irrevocable damage is done, and the whole machine has to be thrown on the scrap heap. God built guilt into our systems to act like that red light. Untreated sin is fatally dangerous to us, because it cuts us off from him. On the other hand, guilt can be instantly removed by 'calling in the expert', God himself. He really can set us free from guilt, and it seems such a tragedy that so many people struggle with it unnecessarily.

Pat was told her guilt was 'all part of grieving', so for four years it spoilt her happiness completely. Her first marriage had been a disaster, and it was only for the children's sake that she and Reg had remained under the same roof. When he died suddenly in his early forties, Pat was able to marry a man she had secretly loved for ten years. 'On paper' this new marriage looked perfect, but something seemed to be making Pat edgy and depressed.

'I keep thinking I've got no right to be happy,' she told a friend who was a social worker.

'Guilt is such a self-indulgent emotion,' replied her friend. The comment did not help Pat at all – it left her feeling guilty for feeling guilty! In desperation she began to attend a nearby church, and the minister was finally able to help her. Under all that false guilt lay a genuine need to be forgiven for her part in the unhappy relationship. Pat had always seen herself as the 'injured party' in her first marriage, blaming everything that went wrong on to Reg. She had not allowed herself to feel a single qualm about deceiving him with her secret affair. She was greatly helped by writing a list of all the ways in which she felt she had failed Reg – the sheer length of the list astonished her – and once she was able to ask for forgiveness, all her long-denied guilt was gone. 'I suddenly feel like

> *But if we confess our sins to God . . . he will forgive us our sins and purify us from all our wrongdoing.* (1 John 1:9, GNB)

it's spring,' she said, when she gave her testimony in church the morning she was baptised.

## When We Break the 'Teapot' Ourselves

What about the guilt someone feels when he or she *is* responsible for a terrible tragedy?

'I met my friend on the way back from the shops and we got talking. I was feeling fed up that day, what with the baby crying all night and Tim grizzling all day. Tim was just three, and he hated me talking to my friends. He started pulling at my skirt – pestering to go home – and I got cross. He started mucking round on the pavement with her two kids, who were a lot older than Tim. The next thing I remember was that awful screech of brakes behind me. I should have kept watching him; I knew that road was dangerous. I'll never forgive myself.'

For five years after Tim's funeral Janet hardly left her house. All the things she had once enjoyed, she felt she should no longer do, but of course she gave herself other reasons for giving them up. Watching television made her eyes hurt, gardening strained her back, knitting was too tiring, and she never felt well enough to make love. In fact, she never felt well at all. The doctor could find no physical reason for that, but subconsciously she felt she had no right to be happy or healthy ever again – since it was her inattention that cost Tim his life.

So how did Janet walk out of the ruins of her 'teapot'? Only one person was willing to go on being Janet's friend, in spite of constant rebuffs, and that was Sue, who was a Christian. Gradually she helped Janet to see that Jesus stepped down into our world so that we need not be destroyed by guilt. Janet had always thought of Jesus as 'a good man' who showed us what God was like, so she was startled when Sue explained who he really was.

> *Sometimes we remain unhealed because we nurture the picture of ourselves as victim and the other as monster, we are disturbed when we see that we too may need to be forgiven for nursing our bitterness and in some cases building a whole life-style around it.* (Russ Parker)

'People began to be angry with him for claiming to be God by saying he could forgive sins,' Sue told her. 'So they killed him, but he did not need to die. It was not some terrible accident: he planned it all in advance. At any moment while they were beating him, punching him and hammering great iron nails through his hands and feet, he could have summoned billions of angels to his rescue, but he chose to remain suspended up there in agony on the cross until the torture ended in his death. He did all that because he wanted to lift all our guilt away by taking the punishment that really ought to have been ours for all the things we regret. He took the rap so we could be free.'

It took Janet months to absorb it all, but Sue 'fed truth to her with a teaspoon' and slowly Janet realised that Jesus did not want her to go on carrying that terrible load of shame and reproach. He wanted her to:

- bring it to him
- tell him about it, holding nothing back
- tell him how sorry she was
- give him the whole lot – and then let it go
- receive his forgiveness
- walk away free, leaving it all with him

Janet was sitting in Sue's garden one hot summer's afternoon when she finally made her once-and-for-all transaction. She gave to Jesus all her guilt, and then received in return his forgiveness – and it was done, for ever.

'It's over,' she said with a deep sigh of relief, and she lay back in her deckchair and allowed the sun to bathe her in warmth. 'It feels like God's love pouring all over me,' she said happily. 'I never need to feel bad like that again.'

---

*At last he came to his senses and said, '. . . I will get up and go to my father and say, Father, I have sinned against God and against you. I am no longer fit to be called your son . . .' He was still a long way from home when his father saw him; his heart was filled with pity, and he ran, threw his arms round his son, and kissed him.* (Luke 15:17–20, GNB)

## How Do We Know We Did It Right?

Repentance and receiving forgiveness are internal and happen secretly in our hearts, and therefore some of us need to do something external and tangible to prove to ourselves that it has happened. Once I was feeling very bad about something particularly nasty that I had done, and somehow a muttered 'Sorry Lord, please forgive me' just did not seem enough. So I wrote a long letter to the Lord, describing it all in detail and how I felt about it. Then I got in the car and drove 10 miles to Mayfield, the beautiful Sussex village where we used to live before I was ill.

In the churchyard stands a huge wooden cross that has always been one of my 'special places'. Carrying my letter, I walked very slowly up to the cross and knelt down in its shadow. Then I read my letter out loud to the Lord, and after I had received his forgiveness I added, 'I'm going to leave all this guilt here with you now, Lord, and when I walk away I won't take it with me.' So I screwed up the piece of paper tightly and buried it in the loose earth at the foot of the cross. When I finally drove home I felt wonderful, and every time I was tempted to feel guilty about that same old sin, I remembered I had left it behind, buried for ever.

### *Beware of the fire alarm!*

Some people set light to their letters and lists, or even flush them down the loo. One friend of mine tied hers round a rock and hurled it into the sea. Others have used a stone to represent all the things they are ashamed of, and when they have confessed them, they drop the stone over a cliff or throw it away in the dustbin.

All these 'visual aids' are helpful, but a friend of ours once had a very embarrassing moment after using one of them. George teaches RE in a boarding school for girls, and one day he was trying to explain what happens to our sins at the cross. The class compiled a list of all the things they wanted to 'dump', and George stuck the paper on a metal cross that stood on his desk, and then set light to it. He hardly had time to blow out the match before the smoke alarms

---

*Our love for him comes as a result of his loving us first.* (1 John 4:19, LB)

went off, and within minutes the entire school, several hundred strong, was lined up neatly in the courtyard while four fire engines hurtled up the school drive. Poor George had a terrible time explaining things to the Fire Chief!

### *Finding someone to witness the transaction*

Finding another person to act as a witness often helps to make this invisible give-and-take feel more real. James 5:16 tells us, 'Confess your sins to one another and pray for one another, so that you will be healed' (GNB). Even though we know it is Jesus who forgives our sins, we cannot see or hear him, so it can help to have someone there to represent him. This person listens to our confession on his behalf, then tells us in words we can hear that we really are forgiven. Finally, he or she prays for healing for us and for others from the wounds our sins have caused. Knowing that our witness believes we are really forgiven helps us should the flames of our own faith flicker in a draught of doubt.

### Fighting Feelings with Faith

Our faith does flicker. Our minds tell us we are forgiven instantly when we repent, but we don't find it so easy to *feel* forgiven. A man who has had his leg amputated often goes on feeling pain in that leg long after it has been removed. He knows that his knee or his foot isn't there any more, but it can take quite a long time for his mind to realise that. The same applies to guilt. It is this clash of faith and feelings that most of us find so difficult, so here are a few methods that people have found helpful in retraining their minds and emotions:

> *The Lord is merciful and loving, slow to become angry and full of constant love. He does not keep on rebuking; he is not angry for ever . . . As far as the east is from the west, so far does he remove our sins from us. As a father is kind to his children, so the Lord is kind to those who honour him.* (Ps. 103:8–13, GNB)

1. Talking to yourself is not always a sign of madness; it can actually help to 'reprogramme' the mind. If we are told something often enough and firmly enough, we soon begin to believe it. Telling ourselves is just as effective! So try talking under your breath to these feelings of guilt. Whenever they bother you, say, 'I am *not* guilty any more. Jesus took all that blame when he died for me. I am free of whatever I did, or fear that I did.'
2. Another excellent way of combating the guilt waves is to turn them instantly into a prayer of gratitude by saying, 'Thank you, Jesus, for dying to rescue me from these horrible feelings.'
3. A friend of mine who was having a terrible job kicking his guilt habit wrote this on a large piece of paper: 'If we confess our sins to God, he will keep his promise and do what is right: he will forgive us our sins and purify us from all our wrongdoing' (1 John 1:9, GNB). Every morning when he got out of bed, he claimed the promise by standing on the piece of paper and repeating the verse out loud, then he added, 'I am forgiven, regardless of how I feel, because God said I am and he's never broken a single promise yet.' Doing something physical like that helped him to realise his freedom was real.
4. Living with someone who constantly abuses us verbally can be devastating, but some people endure it *from themselves*. An internal abusive voice keeps up a continuous tirade of accusations. 'Look at the mess you've made of your life. You're useless! You've blown it so often you can't expect God to forgive you yet again.' We simply do not have to put up with abuse like that. We should tell that invisible bully that Jesus does not think we are worthless. He told us to forgive our brother seventy times seven, so it stands to reason he's going to do even better himself!

## Beware of the 'Hold Up' Factor

Once I rescued a little field mouse just as he was about to be mauled by our ginger cat. I scooped him up, physically unharmed, and

> *God cannot work His greatest good in a heart that harbours a grudge. Grace may flow like a river, but a grudge in your heart may well dam the stream.* (Selwyn Hughes)

carried him back to his cornfield in an empty Marmite jar. Even when he was safely on the ground in familiar territory, he still stayed inside the darkness of the jar, shivering with fright because he could not believe he was really free to live again. It is tragic that so many Christian people seem to remain permanently trapped by guilt because they are never quite sure they are forgiven.

One evening I was asked to speak on the subject of 'Peace in a Troubled World' to a ladies' coffee club. I arrived at the hall, nervous as usual, and sat down in the front row beside a red and grey wheelchair, very like the one I used to have myself. I was soon talking to its occupant, Monika, who was one of those chirpy people, always ready with bright smile or a joke. Yet I sensed that her cheerfulness was only a mask, and it was a real effort to keep it fixed in place.

The time came at last to climb on to the rickety platform and give the talk, and after it was over quantities of homemade cakes and clotted cream were served by way of a reward to the long-suffering audience! I did a lightning calorie count, and decided to flee temptation by going back to find Monika – and it was then that I discovered her mask had slipped. It was rather unnerving to look suddenly right inside the real person. She seemed to want to talk, even though I guessed she had not found talking about *real* things easy for a very long time.

She told me she had been a 'manse kid', for her father was a Baptist minister. 'People put me on a pedestal; they used to say to their children, "Why can't you be good like Monika, the minister's daughter?" I hated it because I knew I wasn't good at all. I did all the right things, sang in the choir, and taught in the Sunday School, but when I was nineteen I discovered I was pregnant. I felt terrible. I really loved my dad – he was such a kind man. I knew what this would do to him. It was a country community, everyone would know. He would feel shamed in front of the whole district. I felt I couldn't do that to him so . . . so, I got rid of it.'

Her voice trailed away in a mist of unshed tears and she sat looking at me helplessly. 'I regretted it as soon as it was done,' she continued at last. 'I felt such a terrible feeling of loss. I've never had another baby. A few months later I found out about the MS. That

*The more we see our sinfulness, the more we see God's abounding grace forgiving us.* (Rom. 5:20, LB)

was my punishment, wasn't it, being stuck in this wheelchair? A life sentence, but it's what I deserve.'

As Monika was talking I had been going cold all over. Suddenly, I could not keep silent any longer.

'Monika,' I said gently. 'You couldn't possibly think that God would send a horrible thing like multiple sclerosis as a punishment, could you?'

'Why not?' she said dully. 'I killed my baby just because I was ashamed to own it.'

'But Monika, you told me you were a "manse kid" – your father was a minister. Surely you must have heard him explain that Jesus took the punishment for *everything* and *anything* we could ever do wrong? Haven't you ever asked him to forgive you?'

'Of course I have!' she retorted furiously. 'Every time I've been in a church since. But he still hasn't forgiven me.'

'But he forgave you the very first time you asked him,' I told her. 'In fact, you've been forgiven for years. God punished *Jesus* for that abortion, so he would not punish you as well by sending the MS. You are forgiven regardless of whether you feel forgiven or not.' Then I found myself saying, 'Perhaps you just couldn't forgive yourself!'

Slowly, a tinge of colour began to seep into Monika's white cheeks. Her smile followed – and this time it was a real smile that came from deep inside her, not a mask that was just stuck on the outside. I wish I had a photograph of how she looked at that moment.

'So the MS just happened,' she said. 'It wasn't God's judgement after all.' At that point, the caretaker came over to us and jangled his keys menacingly. Nearly everyone else had gone home long ago.

As I was helping her into her specially adapted car, she looked up at me and said, 'Yes, you're right. I couldn't forgive myself – in fact, I almost *wanted* to be punished. Perhaps I wouldn't let Jesus take the punishment because I felt I ought to suffer myself. What a fool I've been!' I have not met Monika again since then, but I did speak to her minister's wife about a year later.

'She's like a different person since that long talk you two had in the village hall,' she told me. 'She never seemed to be able to accept the

All who will take God's gift of forgiveness and acquittal are kings of life because of this one man, Jesus Christ. (Rom. 5:17, LB)

MS before; it always made her a bit bitter under all that cheerfulness. But she's thrown herself into life since then. She goes to the local MS group, and is really using it as a means to reach out to others.

People say 'I'll never forgive myself for this' after some tragedy – and the world also expects us to have that kind of attitude. They feel, as we often do, that we have no right to be happy after damaging someone else's happiness. God knows we don't deserve to be happy either, but because he longs for us to be happy, he has taken the blame and the shame that we deserve and put them on to Jesus instead. When we insist on punishing ourselves, we are really insulting him by refusing the precious gift of happiness that cost Jesus so much. The trouble for many people is possibly because they are not quite sure that God really loves them personally.

### The Challenge

Perhaps God could be asking us these questions:

- 'Do you really believe that I love you?'
- 'Do you believe that you do not have to earn my love, and that I do not withhold my love until I have made you more worthy of it?'
- 'Do you believe you are safe in my love, so there is nothing you could ever do that would stop me loving you?'
- 'Do you believe that my love for you is personal, and not simply part of a vague benevolence for all human beings? That it is you, yourself, that I love, and that I have even numbered all the hairs on your head?'

If you have any hesitation over answering 'yes' to any of these questions, turn to page 142 and you might discover why.

### What About the Person We Hurt?

Does our forgiveness from God depend on our saying 'sorry' to the person we hurt? Definitely not, because in certain cases it would be

---

*Right actions in the future are the only true apology for wrong actions in the past*. (David Augsburger)

impossible, or even unwise, to do so. I think, however, that God wants to see on our part a *willingness* to apologise, to restore the relationship and, where possible, to make restitution.

There is no doubt that when we can manage to say we are sorry, we so often take a huge leap forward in our relationship with God – and experience a tremendous release of joy. Maureen, a friend of mine, saw that happen in a rather special way.

She was in her home one afternoon with only her cleaning lady. She had always had a terrible fear of being burgled, so it felt like a nightmare come true when two men pretending to be window cleaners forced their way into the house. They dragged both women into the kitchen, gagged them, then threw them roughly to the floor and tied them to the leg of the table. The beautiful house was ransacked, and everything that was valuable was loaded into the 'window cleaners' van and driven away. When Maureen's husband discovered the two women, they had been left for five hours struggling to breathe through their tight gags, and were stiff, cold and in pain from their many bruises.

The police caught the two men and they were eventually found guilty and sentenced, but Maureen had been so badly shaken by the whole incident that she was ill for a long time afterwards. She was a Christian, but the very thought of trying to forgive her attackers was difficult. Her vicar suggested that it might help her struggle if she began to pray for them, and this she did every morning for the next two years. Then one day she received this remarkable letter:

Dear Mrs Parkside,
I am one of the men who did that break-in at your house. Since I've been in here, I have received a lot of help from the chaplain. I now feel I want to become a committed born-again Christian. He feels it might be a good idea if I wrote and told you that I am very sorry for frightening you that day. I hope you will forgive me.

Maureen was thrilled, and she was able to visit the prison and meet her attacker, whose Christian faith has been flourishing ever since. Incidentally, Maureen's health steadily improved from the time she began praying for her burglars.

> *There is now no condemnation for those who are in Christ Jesus.* (Rom. 8:1, NIV)

That was a story with a happy ending, but on certain occasions it can be sheer self-indulgence to dump our guilt and pain on someone we have seriously sinned against when they knew nothing of it beforehand. There are no absolute rules, because people are all different, so it is vital to seek the advice of someone wise before doing anything hastily.

### It can be risky

There is a particular risk involved when the victim is not yet willing to forgive us. A friend of ours had been having a long-standing disagreement with an older member of his church, who he had always accused of being a 'stick in the mud' and holding the whole church back from blessing. The argument had been rumbling on for a long time, but our friend began to feel sure that the Lord was showing him that he had hurt the other man a great deal over the years. He even began to see that what he had thought was his zeal for God could have been youthful arrogance, and his tactlessness had started the whole row in the first place. So very nervously he went round to his 'enemy's' house and gingerly rang the doorbell.

'I've just popped round to say I'm sorry for all the distress I must have caused you,' he said, when the door opened.

The old man glared down at him from the step and replied, 'Well, it's about time too! And while you're here there's a few things I'd like to get off my chest.' Half-an-hour later he was still talking.

Our friend managed to react in a very Christ-like way by shutting his mouth tight and refusing to defend himself (see Matt. 27:14), but when the old man finally drew breath, he looked at him directly and said, 'Look, I'm really sorry, but all I can say is, please will you forgive me?'

A second later the door was slammed in his face, and he crawled home wishing he had never gone round there in the first place. Did he do the right thing by 'going to his brother'? At the time, he may not have thought so, but looking back a year later, he could see that his spiritual life, which had been drab and dull for a long time, suddenly sprang back into life after that painful interview.

### Danger! High risk of infection!

That incident taught me that there are few things calculated to make anyone feel more of a fool than asking forgiveness and having the request ignored or refused. At best it leaves us with a sense of loss and incompleteness, and at worst we can become so hurt and bitter we 'catch' our victim's unforgiving attitude. Perhaps when we have done everything on our part to put matters right and the person still won't forgive, then we just have to remember that it then becomes his or her problem, not ours. We are free of it for ever.

---

## A Meditation

He never intended to be dishonest, but the expenses of keeping up such a high position were enormous. They had to have a house close to the palace, and a large one at that, because of all the parties and official receptions they needed to give. Then there was the estate up in the Judean hills – they had to have that to escape when pressures at work were high, and of course the children needed seaside holidays, so the house by Lake Galilee was vital. His wife needed expensive clothes and jewellery to maintain their status, and the cost of keeping thousands of slaves and servants was astronomical. None of it could be avoided, but paying for it all was a nightmare.

At first he only 'borrowed' occasionally from the King's accounts. Juggling figures from one ledger to another was easy for him – he was in charge of all the royal finance – and naturally he meant to pay everything back. However, as the children grew larger, so did the bills, and he was dipping deeper and deeper into the King's exchequer. He was far too important for anyone to check up on him, and the King himself was away abroad most of the time.

Then came the day when he realised that his debt was so enormous that he could not repay it even if he sold everything he had, and it would no longer be possible to conceal the deficit when the King next returned home.

He sat in his marble office shaking with fear. He was ruined. He would lose everything and he faced nothing now but public disgrace and death in the debtors' prison. The awful thought of that dark, airless dungeon under the royal barracks kept him awake all that night. He had only been there once, but the memory haunted him still: hundreds of people herded together on straw like animals, trampling their own filth; naked in the darkness and the suffocating stench; dying of disease and starvation.

No! The prospect was appalling. His wife would be dragged there with him while the children would be sold as slaves. When he thought of what that would mean for his beautiful daughters, he gave up the pretence of sleep and paced up and down trying to make a plan. He must do something quickly – pay it back somehow. However, that morning the King returned unexpectedly and sent for the accounts. It was too late! The chancellor's time had run out. As he stood beside the King, watching as he worked slowly through the ledgers, he felt sick with apprehension.

'Guards!' The inevitable had happened: the debt was discovered. The soldiers had almost reached him, but just before he felt their hands seize him he flung himself down before the white marble throne.

'Please, Sire, show mercy!' he cried desperately. 'Give me time to pay!'

At first, as he huddled there, cringing on the floor, he thought the stress must have affected his mind. What he was hearing could not possibly be true. The footsteps of the guards died away into the distance, and he thought he heard the King's voice say,

'I forgive, let's forget all about it.' He was sure he was imagining it until he felt a hand gently pulling him to his feet. 'Come on, my friend,' smiled the King. 'We've got work to do, let's get back to these accounts.'

'Sire,' stammered the chancellor, 'I owe you millions.'

'I know,' said the King, 'but I said, let's forget it.'

'But surely you can't still want me to work for you?'

The King looked straight into his eyes and replied, 'I have forgiven you so much that I am sure you will serve me loyally for ever more.' The chancellor knelt once again, but this time it was to kiss the King's hand.

'I will always obey you, Sire,' he muttered.

'Will you?' replied the King softly. 'Then remember I want you to treat other people as I have treated you.'

'I will!' promised the chancellor, and backed out of the state apartments on a pair of very unsteady legs.

Home through the palace gardens he ran, bathed in sunshine and euphoria. It was springtime, and the world was full of flowers and new green hope for the future. He could live in peace again, free of the threat of slavery and that ghastly debtors' dungeon.

'It's all right!' he shouted, as he burst into his wife's bedroom, 'We're saved!'

She looked up at him crossly from the couch where she was

reclining, 'What on earth do you mean?' He had forgotten that she knew nothing about his debts, and as he told her the whole story he could see she did not believe him.

'You've been drinking again,' she said scornfully. 'The King would never write off a debt as big as that.'

'But he said he would!'

'He said he would,' she mimicked. 'And you believed him?'

'Well . . . yes,' he faltered uncertainly.

'You stupid man! You'll see, he'll go off again on his travels, and when he comes back he'll have changed his mind completely. Once he's had time to think, he'll realise what a fool he would be to trust a man like you. Why, you're nothing but a nasty little thief – why should he ever trust you again?'

'What shall I do?' he mumbled as he flopped down into a chair beside her.

'Raise the money to pay it all back, of course!' she snapped. 'And do it *quick*! You're supposed to be a financial genius, so start making some clever investments. We'll live simply for a while, and then when the King next comes home you can present him with his money.'

'If he hasn't changed his mind, he could be very insulted,' said the chancellor, as he remembered the way the King had smiled at him that morning. Then he added rather wistfully, 'He did *say* he'd forgiven me.'

'You've only got his word for that,' said his wife sharply.

As he walked back again through the palace gardens, he did not notice the flowers or the spring sunshine. His head was bent in thought as a thousand schemes chased themselves round his brain. Only the day before he had been asked to finance an expedition to discover new diamond mines in Ethiopia. There was a double fortune to be made, but he would have to raise the capital quickly before anyone else heard about it. 'I'll close on everyone who owes me a single groat,' he thought grimly. Just then, he looked up to see one of his young scribes hurrying towards him. 'And here's the first bird for plucking. He doesn't owe me much, but he'll serve as an example to the others, and frighten them into paying up quickly.'

'You have a debt to pay, young man,' he said sternly. The scribe had asked him for the loan a couple of years before. He was getting married and wanted to buy a small house. He should have had time enough to pay it back by now; but the young man's face turned white.

'Sir,' he said, 'please give me a little more time, my wife has just had our first baby and there were so many expenses. I'll pay you very soon, I promise.' But the chancellor lunged at him and grabbed him by the throat.

'I want that money by tomorrow morning!' he roared. 'Tomorrow – or else . . .'

'Sir, please, not the debtors' prison . . . my wife . . . the child?' He had fallen to his knees in the pathway and the chancellor had to step on to the grass to avoid him as he swept towards the palace. It was all most distasteful, but it had to be done – it was just part of the business world.

However, the young scribe was well liked in court circles and his wife was very beautiful. People felt outraged at the sight of them being hauled away by the guards as the bailiffs invaded their home. The plaintive cries of the baby added a final touch of pathos to the story that was soon buzzing about the palace. When the chancellor began demanding money from all and sundry, his already waning popularity plummeted and the indignation of the entire palace staff rose against him.

'Fancy treating his own scribe like that! Someone ought to make a complaint to the King!' And someone did.

'How could you do such a thing?' It was a very different royal face that confronted the chancellor now.

You can read how the story ended in Matthew 18:32–35 (GNB): ' "You worthless slave!" he said. "I forgave you the whole amount you owed me, just because you asked me to. You should have had mercy on your fellow-servant, just as I had mercy on you." The King was very angry, and he sent the servant to jail to be punished . . . And Jesus concluded, "That is how my Father in heaven will treat every one of you unless you forgive your brother from your heart." '

If only the chancellor could have believed he had really been let off his debt, he would have been able to let others off their debts to him. In this story, was Jesus saying that when we believe God has forgiven us for so much, then the comparatively small wrongs that others do to us will be easy to forgive?


## A Prayer

*'Come to me all you who are tired of carrying a heavy load of shame and humiliation for "I am He who blots out and cancels your transgressions, and I will remember your sins no more".'* (Isa. 43:25, AMP)

Lord Jesus, I can't look up into your face. I feel too dirty, shameful, disgusting. My soul feels violated. I have been shamed, exposed and humiliated. I've got nowhere left to hide now everyone knows. I feel they blame me for what happened, and I'm always conscious of them whispering and looking at me oddly.

*'Come to me, for they said of me, "He had no dignity or beauty . . . We despised him and rejected him . . . we ignored him as if he were nothing. But he endured the suffering that should have been ours . . . Because of our sins he was wounded, beaten because of the evil we did. We are healed by the punishment he suffered, made whole by the blows he received".'* (Isa. 53:2–5, GNB)

Help me to look up at you. I know your body was abused and ill-treated by people who did not care what they were doing to you. You were left to hang up there, naked and exposed, while people stared curiously at you. People blame me for things that weren't my fault, but that is what they were doing to you too. Scornful faces and reproachful eyes surrounded you as well.

Help me to remember that although you were shamed up there on the cross, you were never shameful. Help me to remember that although I may be shamed, I am not shameful either, because you have made me pure and clean by what you did for me on that cross. I give you my wretchedness, so you can hold it with your own, and in exchange I receive your purity and innocence. I do not deserve it, but I receive it with grateful joy.

### Perhaps the Lord Might Respond Like This

'You are precious in my sight, and honoured, and I love you' (Isa. 43:4, AMP).

## STOP FOR A MOMENT

*I constantly meet active and enthusiastic Christians who secretly admit that they have never felt sure that God really loves them. That was my problem once, and I always ask them this question: 'How did you get on with your parents?'*

*As we grow up, we seem to paint ourselves a portrait of God that looks a lot like the adults who were important to us as children. We think he will treat us as they always did. These personalised pictures are always inaccurate, because none of us was brought up by perfect people, yet we seem to base our concept of God's character on them rather than on the Bible, and end up with a distorted view of what he is like.*

*Try going through the following checklist and see if you can spot yourself:*

- *Were your parents angry and abusive? Did you sometimes even suspect that they enjoyed hurting you? If so, you may find it difficult to be sure that God is not waiting round the corner ready to 'get you' or watching your pain from a distance with his arms folded.*
- *Did your parents love you, but feel it right to punish you often? If so, you may find it terribly hard to believe God really has forgiven your sin without* punishing you first.
- *Did they have impossibly high standards for you? Were they only pleased with you when you achieved high marks at school and won every possible race on sports day? Did you only feel worthy of their love when you were clean, quiet and being extremely good? If so, you may struggle constantly to please God, but never quite feel that you have. Perhaps you are the kind of person who can't say 'no' to any request for help and goes dashing around trying to do good, kind things in the hope that the more you achieve for God, the more he will love you.*
- *Were your parents very busy people who were always hurrying off to do important things somewhere else? Were you never allowed to 'bother' your father with your little concerns? If so, you may think of God as cold, distant and remote, far too high above you to care how you feel.*
- *Were your parents moody, changeable and inconsistent? Perhaps one day they seemed to love you, and the next you were just in the way. If so, you may have a problem believing that God's love is changeless.*

- *Were your parents very loving people who were always looking after the needs of others in the caring professions, the church or at home with numerous brothers and sisters? If so, you may always feel that God must care far more about people who have big problems, so that you should not take up his time with your smaller worries.*
- *Did your parents split up? Perhaps the one you loved the most left and you felt abandoned? If so, you may find it hard to feel sure that God will not suddenly drop you.*
- *Did your parents adore you, sacrifice everything and everyone else for your needs, and fall over themselves running around to gratify your smallest whim? Did their whole existence revolve around you and you alone? If so, you may find it hard to accept that God loves you enough to say 'no' to your demands sometimes. To you, being loved always meant being given exactly what you wanted, so when things go wrong now you automatically think you have lost God's love.*

*We do not have to be bound by the erroneous thought patterns we inherited from childhood. It is vital that we chuck away these counterfeit portraits of God, and begin looking at the genuine picture that the Bible paints. If you are still struggling over all this, try repeating one of the following verses three times a day – it's a bit like taking medicine!*

*I have loved you with an everlasting love; I have drawn you with lovingkindness.* (Jer. 31:3, NIV)

*I will never leave you; I will never abandon you.* (Heb. 13:5, GNB)

*Can a mother forget the baby at her breast and have no compassion on the child she has borne? Though she may forget, I will not forget you!* (Isa. 49:15, NIV)

# 8

# QUESTIONING AND BARGAINING

When Babs lost her nineteen-year-old son in a motorbike crash, it was yet another chapter in a whole series of disasters that had been hitting her family for the last three years.

'Why should it all happen to such nice people?' Everyone in the district seemed to be saying something like that, and when Babs went to see her vicar she was certainly right in the middle of the stage of questioning and bargaining.

'Life's just one gigantic "Why?"' she said miserably. 'Sometimes I think the Lord must be testing us – trying to teach us something. And that makes me furious. Why should my son lose his life just so I'll learn something I didn't want to learn anyway? But then I tell myself that God doesn't do horrid things like that, so it must be Satan attacking us. That makes me scared stiff, because if he's running amok, then what's he going to do to us next? Someone suggested a curse might have been put on the family, and yet another friend was convinced that it was all because of some sin in a previous generation. I'm so confused. I keep saying to the Lord, "I'll do anything you want, go anywhere you like, but just don't let anything else go wrong for our family."'

> *Thousands follow Christ when he gives them what they want, few follow him when he confronts them with what he wants.* (Selwyn Hughes)

## The Law of Cause and Effect

Poor Babs, she was hurting so badly, and groping around desperately for an explanation. Most of us human beings feel safer and more in control of our lives if we can provide neat answers for everything that happens. Right from our earliest childhood, 'why' and 'because' go hand in hand:

'Don't touch the fire.'

'Why?'

'Because it will burn you.'

As adults, we feel that if we could only discover the cause of our problems, we might be able to put things right – or at least avoid it happening again.

So naturally anyone going through the Broken Teapot Syndrome is full of questions, but so often there are no easy answers to life's greatest tragedies. When insurance companies can't find a culprit to blame for a disaster they call it an 'act of God', but for people who believe in a God of tenderness and compassion that answer creates a thousand new questions.

'Surely he couldn't be behind all this?' we think, as we frantically clutch at our disappearing faith. 'I wouldn't put my worst enemy through such misery – and God is supposed to love me.'

Perhaps people with a strong faith find this stage of the grieving process even more difficult than it would be, say, for an atheist. We believe that God is in control of the universe and also the tiniest details of our lives, so why, when he has the power to protect us, has he allowed all this to happen? The stage of questioning can feel like a terrible onslaught to our faith, just at a time when we are most vulnerable.

## We May Ask Questions

We must give ourselves permission to ask 'Why?' because God does not want mechanical robots or mindless 'yes men'. We also need to let ourselves feel the confusion and the frustration, and not bottle it all up with a label saying 'Poison, do not touch'. God gave us minds,

*Seek his face and not his hand.* (R.T. Kendall)

and we should use them – instead of passively accepting the party line of our particular church circle.

It can be destructive to go round asking numerous different people, 'Why is this happening to me?' They will all be happy to tell you (in fact, many won't even wait for you to ask), and they will all give you advice on how to put things right. The only problem will be that all their opinions may be different, and if you try to follow all their suggestions you will soon feel demented! (I know, I fell into this trap myself!)

As I have said before, a Christian counsellor or your own minister is probably the best person to help, because there may well be things you need to discover. God never sends these calamities to punish us, but he can use them to open our eyes to sins that we may have buried away, unconfessed. Sometimes there is another cause that his power can deal with, such as a curse, occult interference or some binding from past generations. These things are worth investigating because they can so easily be removed by God's power.

## When Questions Become Dangerous

Yet there is a point when we have to realise that while we stand on this earth, bound by the limits of time, we shall never be able to see human suffering from God's perspective. Many people have tried to do so and written books on their conclusions, but all they can really offer us are tiny fragments of truth. The questioning stage begins to become dangerous when a person begins to spend too much time and energy dashing here and there after these fragments, because if their search goes on too long they could lose sight of God in a dry, intellectual maze of theological theories.

## The Challenge

In this stage, perhaps the Lord is asking us: 'Will you trust me without any explanations?'

*You may yourself ebb and flow, rise and fall, wax and wane, but your Lord is this day as he was yesterday.* (Samuel Rutherford)

Dr Helen Roseveare had spent many years establishing a hospital in the remote rainforests of what was then the Belgian Congo. The health of thousands of people was improved by her work and many lives saved. Then in 1964, during the vicious civil war, her hospital was attacked and she herself was brutally beaten and raped. She was forced to return to Britain, and her work at the mission station was left in ruins for a long time.

She was a Cambridge graduate, a scientist with a brilliant mind, and had been trained to look for answers. So naturally she asked God why he had allowed all that to happen, and she felt that she received this response from him: 'Will you trust me if I never tell you why?' Dr Roseveare's acceptance of that tantalising challenge was a profound help in the development of her personal relationship of trust in God, and through sharing it in her books and talks it has blessed many others.

Although questions are normal, therefore, there has to come a time when we let them go and realise that we will never understand God – he would not be God if we could. Our human intellects are too small to reach him, but we can reach him by faith. Of course, our faith is also too small to reach him, but once he sees the tiniest spark, he adds to it until we have all we need.

Through all our questioning he says, 'I do not expect you to understand me, but I do expect you to trust me.' If we can manage to make that quantum leap of faith, all our questions can be turned round to produce a huge growth spurt of faith that will benefit us eternally.

## Beware of the 'Hold Up' Factor

If at the end of all the questions we conclude that it was all God's fault, we might decide to blame him for all that has happened, and angrily exclude him from our lives for ever more.

The 'hold up' factor in this stage is a permanent resolve never to forgive God, which results in a total breakdown in the relationship.

*Change and decay in all around I see, oh thou who changes not abide with me.* (Henry Francis Lyte)

Letting It All Out

It is vitally important to remember that this permanent anger is not the same as feeling angry with God *sometimes*, and telling him so. Many of the greatest saints in church history have been angry with God – and survived. My favourite, St Teresa of Avila, was on a mission of mercy when, late on a stormy night, her coach was stuck in rising flood water, miles from civilisation. She was elderly and frail, but all night she and her nuns had to tramp through deep mud and driving rain. They were wet, cold and extremely hungry. As usual, St Teresa prayed out loud as she went, but her sisters were amazed (and perhaps relieved) to hear her say to the Lord, 'Well, if this is how you treat your friends, I'm not surprised you have so few!'

Many Bible characters were also honest with God about their feelings. Moses, who spoke to the Lord 'face to face, as a man speaks with his friend' (Exod. 33:11, NIV), obviously felt confident enough in their relationship to say bluntly, 'If you are going to treat me like this, take pity on me and kill me, so that I won't have to endure your cruelty any longer' (Num. 11:15, GNB).

Jeremiah felt utterly let down by God on several occasions, and in Jeremiah 15 he admits that he is angry – and then adds, 'Why do I keep on suffering? Why are my wounds incurable? Why won't they heal? Do you intend to disappoint me like a stream that goes dry in the summer?' (Jer. 15:18, GNB.)

Job, of course, was more outspoken than anyone: 'Listen to my bitter complaint. Don't condemn me, God . . . Is it right for you to be so cruel?' (Job 10:1–3, GNB.) 'Can't you see it is God who has done this? . . . I protest against his violence, but no one is listening . . . God has blocked the way . . . he has hidden my path in darkness. He has taken away all my wealth and destroyed my reputation. He batters me from every side. He uproots my hope and leaves me to wither and die . . . The hand of God has struck me down' (Job 19:6–21, GNB).

Job said a great many other things too, but (as we shall see in the next chapter) anger must be released – it cannot be allowed to become a long-term, deliberate attitude of blame. Job 1:22 tells us

*Jesus Christ is the same yesterday, today, and for ever.* (Heb. 13:8, GNB)

that, 'In spite of everything that had happened, Job did not sin by blaming God' (GNB).

## Is It Wrong to Be Angry with God?

Perhaps we could dare to try to see our anger from God's point of view. In order to do that I have constructed an imaginary situation where one of my children might be extremely angry with me because I have prevented him doing something, or denied him something he wanted very badly. As a loving parent, I could see that what he wanted would be utterly destructive, but that he was too young to appreciate the sensible reason for my refusal. I love him so much I would be very sad that he did not trust me, but I would accept that his angry reaction was normal – so long as he expressed it correctly – and soon.

(a) If, however, the anger remained for many months, and he expressed it by locking himself away in his room in a world of brooding, resentful silence, and refused to speak to me or anyone else in the family, I should be most concerned.

(b) He could do me a lot of damage if he stormed off to express his anger to other people, telling our friends at church all kinds of things they never knew about me before!

(c) I would be terribly upset if he diverted the anger he felt towards me on to other members of the family and started punching the smaller ones, kicking the cat, or even smashing the china.

(d) The expression of anger that would hurt me most of all would be if he slammed out of the house in a rage, vowing never to return.

(e) As a parent, I would far prefer him to come to me with his anger direct and tell me how he feels. When my children manage to do that in real life, the whole thing usually blows over quite quickly and finishes with a muttered 'Sorry, Mum' from them and a hug of forgiveness from me.

God is a far better parent than any of us could ever be, so he understands our immaturity and our furious reactions. As Susan

> *Now, Job, make peace with God and stop treating him like an enemy . . .* (Job 22:21, GNB)

Jenkins puts it, 'For we beat upon his breast from within the circle of his arms.'

The following chapter on anger contains some guidelines for expressing our feelings to God, but sometimes we are afraid to do that, so we hold it all in, as in example (a), locking ourselves away from God and others at church while we seethe and simmer internally, and our fellowship with God is suspended. That would hurt him very much because he values that friendship with us so highly.

God's relationship with other people could be damaged by our anger if we expressed it as in example (b), by spreading our doubts and dissatisfactions all round the church and denting other people's faith.

So often we transfer our anger on to others, as in (c), by venting it on them unfairly because we are too afraid to go to God direct. We quarrel with the vicar because he fails to call, or with our friends because they 'don't understand', or we roar at the children and slap the baby. Because God also loves the people we are hurting, it causes him added pain to watch their suffering.

Example (d) is, of course, the 'hold up' factor, and it is the expression of anger God dreads the most, because he longs to turn round in our favour all the suffering we encounter in this life, to transform it for our benefit and for the good of those we love. When we refuse to forgive him, he cannot 'work all things together for good' (Rom. 8:28) and the whole situation becomes destructive.

---

## A Meditation

People described Jo as a self-made man, but he never agreed with them. 'If you give your life to God, he'll always take care of you' was one of Jo's many little 'sayings', and his teenage children always groaned when he trotted it out yet again. But Jo had done exactly that soon after leaving school with no official bits of paper to help him get

---

*Perhaps the issue for Christians is simply this: is God there for me, or am I there for God? Does He exist to do my will or do I exist to do His?* (Justyn Rees)

established. He had taken a job labouring in a building firm, and less than twenty years later he owned the firm – and several others.

'People can always be sure of quality in one of my houses' was another of Jo's sayings, and his success lay in the fact that it was true.

He adored his children, even when they were going through the worst of their teenage rebellion, and he was always up at six in the morning, praying for them each by name – 'Just in case they forget to pray for themselves'. The family home was large and beautiful, but somehow Jo still managed to give thousands away to charity, saying as he wrote the cheques,'The more you give to God, the more God gives to you.'

The rugged world of the building trade respected Jo, but at church he was genuinely loved. 'Jo's a good man, he deserves to be happy,' was a sentiment shared by the whole district.

Then one day, Satan went to see God.

'Where have you been, then?' asked God.

'Oh, just walking about, looking at things,' replied Satan nonchalantly. 'Keeping an eye on the people you call your friends.'

'So you'll have noticed Jo,' said God, with a little smile of pride. 'Now there's a man who really loves me.'

'Well, "loving you" pays him well enough!' replied Satan tartly. 'He knows which side his bread's buttered. Just look what he gets out of it! You can't resist pouring blessings on him, can you? Look at his bank account! And doesn't he love that reputation you've built for him? Everyone asking his advice, and thanking him with tears in their eyes I'm not surprised he loves you!'

God sighed. He knew what Satan had in mind.

'I'll prove to you that your fine friend Jo only loves you for what he gets out of you,' continued Satan with a sneer. 'Let me take it away – everything he values in life. We'll soon see if he loves you then.'

God's heart was heavy. For a long time he had been wanting Jo to have certain special things – precious assets he had not yet been able to give him. However, these treasures could only be discovered in the

---

*When we agree to the disagreeable things in life the life of Christ presses to the fore and the Lord is manifested and glorified through us, and it is then that we become broken bread and poured out wine to feed and nourish others.* (Oswald Chambers)

darkness of adversity (Isa. 45:3). If he let Satan attack Jo, these valuable things could be his. Yet God shrank away from the very thought of it. He loved Jo, he was the very apple of his eye, and even though he could see clearly how much blessing he could bring to Jo's soul through Satan's plans, he still loathed the idea of the pain he must suffer in order to gain the prize.

There was also the very real possibility that he could lose Jo altogether. It was a terrible risk, and not one that God was prepared to take lightly.

'Come on,' said Satan impatiently. 'Why are you holding back? If you know Jo loves you, then you must know he'll trust you.'

With another sigh, God gave Satan the permission he needed.

'But you must not touch him personally,' he warned. Satan nodded, and went away whistling confidently.

'It's only the recession,' Jo told his workforce the day he had to lay off another twenty men. 'Things will soon improve. "The good Lord looks after his own" – that's what I always say.' Yet the work contracts seemed to be drying up completely, while the bills grew bigger by the day.

The offer from the London Consortium looked like the break he had been praying for, but he still spent two days fasting for guidance before he threw in his lot with their venture. He was so sure that he could trust them that he put up his house, and everything he owned, to raise the money he needed to buy himself in on the deal.

The crash came with devastating suddenness. It seemed as if in just one day he had lost his business, his home, his cars and his money, while the humiliation of bankruptcy was staring him in the face. None of that seemed to matter at all when they broke the news to him about the accident. The children had been at one of their wild parties. The building had caught fire, and they were not among the survivors.

At first the shock caused a kind of euphoria. Jo felt he was positively being carried along by the power of God. At the funeral he coined another of his sayings: 'The Lord gave it all to me, he has a perfect right to take it away again.' People quoted that all over

---

*He plied him with many questions, but Jesus gave him no answer.* (Luke 23:9, NIV)

Britain, and even used it in sermons as an example of patience under trial.

'What a good witness Jo is to his faith,' said everyone who knew him.

'There!' said God, next time he saw Satan. 'I told you Jo would never stop loving me.' Satan was still feeling rather sore; his good ideas so often seemed to backfire on him. Perhaps he should make a last attempt?

'Well,' he said with a shrug. 'Jo's a big strong man. He knows he can build his business back with his marvellous reputation. You let me get at him through his health – *then* he'll soon stop trusting you.'

God loathed the very thought of it, but he also knew Jo had not received quite all those good things yet.

'You have my permission,' he said sadly, 'but remember, you may not kill him.'

'It's one of these viruses,' the doctor told Jo's wife Helen. 'He'll get over it.' But Jo did not get over it.

'These things take time,' said the doctor a month later.

One day in August, when five months had elapsed, Helen said, 'Why don't you snap out of this? Get up and find a job! Why should I have to slave away supporting us both while you lie there in bed all day?'

Jo rolled over towards the wall; he could not bear the sight of her vicious face. They were living in a small, two-roomed flat by then, on the shabby side of town, crowded on top of each other until irritation soured their marriage.

'Call yourself a Christian! Fat lot of good all that stuff did you in the end!' He could still hear her voice, even with the pillow over his head. She had never been as committed to church as he had been; now he secretly wondered if she had not been right all along.

When the door slammed behind her at last, he sighed with relief. At least he had eight hours peace from her nagging while she emptied bed pans at the geriatric hospital. What had he done to

---

*Do you know the mind and purposes of God? Will long searching make them known to you? Are you qualified to judge the Almighty? He is as faultless as heaven is high – but who are you? His mind is fathomless – what can you know in comparison?* (Job 11:7–8, LB)

her? he thought, as remorse stabbed him painfully. She hated it there, and earned a smaller pittance than he would once have given his building apprentices. Her hands were as rough as her tongue these days, and she kept saying she wouldn't stick it – or him – much longer. He couldn't blame her!

It was hot at the top of this tower block. The man who built it had been a rival once, and as Jo looked round the shoddy room he reckoned the fool needed shooting. Once he and Helen would have been lying on a beach somewhere, during August heatwaves like this, but now they were forced to sweat the summer out in a jerry-built oven. A fly buzzed against the windowpane and made his headache even worse. Everything ached these days, every joint in his body hurt as he eased his position on the lumpy mattress. He was thirsty, but the physical effort involved in dragging himself to the kitchen next door was too great to consider.

'Why are you doing this to me, God?' he snarled. 'You've taken everything now, haven't you? I hope you're satisfied.' Not even his reputation remained to console him. Some of the people who had lost their jobs or their investments when his business crashed were turning nasty now, calling him a liar and a dishonest hypocrite all round town. They would have sued him if he had anything left to make it worth their while. Worst of all, his Christian friends seemed to believe their accusations, and he even had letters saying this sickness must be God's way of calling him to repentance. His friends had stopped coming round with flowers and cakes, and the phone never rang these days.

'You know for sure that I've never lied or cheated anyone, God,' he raged, 'so why don't you stand up for me?'

Last week the worst had happened: his doctor seemed to lose patience with him. 'I think these symptoms are all in your mind,' he had said. 'The hospital tests are negative. Where's your courage, man? Can't you face up to life? You should get up and take yourself out for some good long walks in the country and stop all this self-pity.'

Jo had been furious. 'Walks in the country? Can't you see I can't

---

*When my thoughts were bitter and my feelings were hurt, I was as stupid as an animal; I did not understand you.* (Ps. 73:21–22, GNB)

even stagger to the toilet without sweating with weakness?'

He'd said a great many other things as well, but of course the doctor had won with his parting remark to Helen as she showed him to the door: 'I'll make an appointment for him with a psychiatrist; it's time we got him back to work.'

Helen had loved it. She'd been on the phone in the next room all that evening and now everyone would know. 'Fancy a man with all that faith sinking as low as that,' they'd all be saying. 'Lying in bed malingering until they had to get a shrink to convince him he was a fraud!'

'You know I'm not making it up!' he muttered towards the cracked plaster of the ceiling. 'Aren't you listening to me any longer?'

At midday the phone rang. Jo was both surprised and pleased, but the struggle into the next room took him so long that it had stopped before he reached it.

As he stood clutching the table and fighting the waves of dizziness, the phone rang once again. It was Bruce, the senior elder at church, but his voice sounded so condescending that he could have been addressing a naughty member of the Sunday School.

'Since we heard how your doc is feeling about you, we've been praying quite a bit,' he began. 'More likely, gossiping,' thought Jo bitterly. 'The other elders and I feel we should come round and see you this evening,' continued Bruce. 'We feel we have various words from the Lord for you. Would eight o'clock be all right?'

'What do they want?' protested Helen when she arrived home. 'I've had a long day, I'm too tired after work to start making tea for that lot.'

'Don't bother then,' snapped Jo, adding crossly, 'I've had a long day too, and I'm tired just from doing nothing.'

'Whose fault's that?' she replied acidly. 'It's time you told all that church lot to get lost, if you ask me.'

'I didn't ask you!' growled Jo, who knew perfectly well he agreed with her.

The four men were looking ominous as they filed into the bedroom. They stood round the bed, gazing down at him without

> *I will give you the treasures of darkness, riches stored in secret places, so that you may know that I am the Lord.* (Isa. 45:3, NIV)

saying anything at all for so long that Jo felt quite unnerved. Who did they think they were, anyway? They had all sat under his preaching for years, and he had picked them out to be elders himself. One of them had worked as his employee, two of the others he had helped out of serious financial difficulties, and he'd led young Graham to the Lord in his own sitting-room.

When he was beginning to think they would never break the silence, they started on him – one after the other.

'We all feel we have different aspects of the truth to share with you, Jo,' began Bruce. 'As a church we have prayed and fasted for you regularly over these months; and, as you know, we have held a special service of healing for you, but we have always been praying for a physical illness. We didn't realise, until we heard that your doctor says . . .'

'I'm making it all up,' put in Jo bitterly.

'Well . . . quite . . . but I feel that all this must be due to some sin you won't face up to. Some dishonest business deal you haven't confessed yet, perhaps?' At the start of his illness Jo had confessed so many things to these four elders that he felt naked every time he thought about it, but it had made no difference to his health. 'Search your heart, Jo,' continued Bruce, 'be honest with us for once.'

'For once!' said Jo. 'God knows I've never been anything else.'

'If God knew that, Jo,' said Bruce, shaking his head sadly, 'surely he would have told us four elders, don't you think?'

'Jo, I feel it's all a matter of faith,' said the man who had been the best chippy Jo had ever employed. 'A man like you ought to have enough faith to tell this sickness to go – instantly.'

'I'm afraid it has something to do with your wife's attitude,' added the third elder, and Jo heard an indignant snort from the far side of the bedroom door. Helen wouldn't like that, he thought grimly.

'Surely you must realise, Jo, that God never wills sickness like this for his children,' said the last man piously. 'He wants us all fit and well and out there serving him. You just don't want to get well, do you? You're not even trying.'

'Yes, but God could be teaching him something,' interrupted Bruce.

---

*Have you ever noticed how the same trouble that turns one Christian sour is used by another to refine and sweeten his life?* (Selwyn Hughes)

'I disagree,' said the fourth man, 'but even if you were right, why doesn't Jo just learn it quick, then he could be better instantly!'

Something inside Jo snapped. He sat up in bed and shouted, 'If it was as easy as that, do you think I'd still be stuck here like this? And if Christianity is all about kicking a man when he's down, you can keep it! You're always coming here with "words from the Lord" for me, but they keep changing! Why can't he make up his mind? Get out of here – and you can tell God from me that if he can't look after me and mine better than this, I'm through with him!'

'Jo!' said Bruce reproachfully, 'perhaps if you stopped treating God like an enemy he might bless you with your health again.'

'Get out!' yelled Jo. 'It's him who's treating me like an enemy, and I've had enough of it!'

Helen had her say as well – once they'd gone – and it developed into the biggest row they'd ever had. The whole 'delightful' evening finished when she packed her bags and left to stay with her best friend Susan.

'You can jolly well look after yourself in the future!' she shouted, as the door slammed with awesome finality.

The night was hot, oppressive with the heavy threat of thunder. Even the irritating fly had abandoned him, and as he lay there in the darkness he had never felt so utterly alone. 'That's it then,' he thought, as somewhere in the distance a church clock struck two. 'There's no one left who cares a rap about me now.'

But that was where Jo was wrong. He was not alone in that hot airless room. If only Jo could have seen the face of God at that moment. It was so close to him, he could have touched it by faith had he tried. The look of anguish would have astonished him. God's compassion longed to reassure Jo and comfort him. His heart was breaking as he watched him lying there.

'Trust me, Jo, please trust me just a little bit longer.' God said it several times, but Jo had lost the knack of listening to his voice.

Satan was watching Jo too, during that fateful August night. He

In a human sense, it is understandable how most of us shrink from disappointment, bereavement and other trials, but in a divine sense, these are the very things that God uses to deepen His work of Grace in our lives. (Selwyn Hughes)

was sitting in the corner of the hot little bedroom smiling in triumph.

'How are the mighty fallen,' he remarked nonchalantly.

'He hasn't reached the crisis yet,' said God. 'You wait.'

'Yes,' said Satan with a cunning smile, 'I can afford to wait.'

'If I could have just five minutes with God,' said Jo out loud. 'By golly, I'd ask him a few questions!'

'Trust me,' urged God silently while Satan smirked.

A sudden feeling of desolation came over Jo.

'If I haven't got God any more, then I've got nowhere left to run,' he muttered.

'Come to me, Jo,' breathed God. 'Trust me just a little bit longer.'

'I keep thinking I hear someone saying, "trust me",' said Jo, poking at his ear crossly. 'P'raps I am going mad after all, and I've started hearing voices.'

'Trust me, Jo.' There it was again.

Jo had the uncanny feeling that God was challenging him. 'Suppose all this happened because he wanted me to trust him – whatever.' Jo pulled himself up the bed a little – he felt he was having some kind of revelation. 'Trust him without any of my props – trust him just because I love him – for himself, and not what he gives me. Suppose that's what he's been after all along?'

'Well Jo?' said God. Heaven waited in breathless suspense and Satan fidgeted restlessly.

'Well, I suppose I might as well trust him,' whispered Jo at last. 'Because I'm darned sure I've got nothing else left but him now.' Then he added slowly, 'But then, maybe if I've got him I don't really need anything else anyway.' He paused, searching his mind for one of his sayings, but for once he failed completely. Then back into his mind came the words of someone else – he was sure he had heard them somewhere before – and he repeated them softly to himself. 'Though he slay me, yet will I trust him,' and 'when he has tried me I shall come forth as gold.'

Jo sat very still; he did not dare to move. God had not answered any of his questions, but suddenly he felt quite overwhelmed by his love. It seemed to pour down on him directly from heaven itself like

> *Let Almighty God be your gold, and let him be silver, piled high for you. Then you will always trust in God and find that he is the source of your joy.* (Job 22:25–26, GNB)

thick, golden liquid. Gradually it filled the room, and swept away everything but its own tremendous reality. Tears seeped from the corners of Jo's eyes and dampened his rugged cheeks.

'Lord,' he whispered, 'I'm so sorry I doubted you. I said some stupid things, didn't I? Honestly, I didn't mean most of it. Forgive me. And I'm sorry I was so angry with them all at church. They didn't mean to be heartless.' He had the oddest feeling that God might be angry with them too, so he hastily added, 'Please forgive them too for not seeing what you were really up to. Don't go punishing them for that – they were only trying to help.'

Then, lying back, Jo closed his eyes and slept like a contented child. He never saw Satan slink away, defeated and shamed. Nor did he see the angels dancing with delight on the scruffy covers of his bed. But all heaven rejoiced that night as he slept, and there was a smile on the face of God.

I am not quite sure how this modern version of the age-old story of Job should end. Jo has to get better, of course, and, if the original story of Job is anything to go by, he becomes a multi-millionaire! I am not sure if even my imagination will allow Helen to have lots more children at her age, but perhaps they could adopt?

However we decide the story should finish, there is one vital fact we must not overlook. Job's fortunes were restored after he had:

- repented of his anger against God (Job 40:3–4; 42:3, 6)
- forgiven God through an experience of renewal (Job 42:5–6)
- forgiven his infuriating friends by praying for them (Job 42:10)

Then, and only then, could his story reach its happy ever after ending. God does not always restore everything to us in a physical sense during this life, but we must reach the same point as Jo before we can emerge whole from our Broken Teapot experiences.

---

*In all the changes, confusion and uncertainty there is only one cast iron fact that we can cling to with perfect confidence. Whatever is happening to us, God can make it all work for our good and the benefit of those we love – if we allow him to do so.* (Jean Rees)

## A Prayer

'*Come to me all you who are tired out from carrying heavy loads full of questions and confusion, for "I alone know the plans I have for you, plans to bring you prosperity and not disaster, plans to bring about the future you hope for".*' (Jer. 29:11, GNB)

'My God, my God, why . . . ?' 'If it is possible, take this cup of suffering away from me . . .' Lord, these are your own words and I echo them, but I also want to reach the point of adding, 'Nevertheless, not my will but thine be done.' I want to stop trying to buy your favour with promises of money, service or good behaviour, to stop trying to manipulate you by prayer, fasting and sacrifice. From now on I want to allow you to have your way in this situation, and use it to bring good things to everyone involved. My Father, I do not understand you, but I trust you.

## Perhaps the Lord Might Respond Like This

'I cannot give you all the answers, because – as a human – your view of the universe is as limited as that of the ant who wriggles between the stalks of grass in a field. From where I am, I can view the whole earth in one glance. I can see the jagged mountain peaks, the quiet rivers and the icebergs floating in dark blue water. I can also see each blade of grass in your field. You feel you are struggling round in circles, but I can see clearly where you are going and each obstacle you will face among the matted roots and muddy soil. How do I explain to you how beautiful the world looks from up here? You could never understand with your limited experience. But one day, when I lift you up here to see it all with me, from my perspective, then you will look back down at your field where you struggle now and laugh at the tiny things you thought were insurmountable. Trust me just a little longer – one day you will see it all, *and* understand.'

---

*And He doesn't explain, He trusts us not to be offended, that's all.* (Amy Carmichael)

## STOP FOR A MOMENT

*Had the real Job been able to see that a spiritual battle was taking place above his suffering, he would no doubt have found the whole thing considerably easier to bear. For us, struggling through our own misery and confusion, we do at least have the benefit of his story. It does not give a complete answer – like all other explanations it is just a fragment of the truth – but it does show us that we are not actually alone.*

*Knowing that, like Job, we are watched by the two Superpowers could make us feel like little pawns in a game they are playing above our heads – until we remember that we decide which of them wins: Satan, when we allow our problems to destroy us; or God, when we allow him to work them all for our good.*

### Warning!

*If you have not yet had time to release your anger fully to the Lord, you may find the following exercise too difficult at present.*

### Take Two Sheets of Paper

*At the top of the first sheet, write 'The Facts', then underneath make a list of everything that happened when your 'teapot' broke – the actual events and the losses they caused. Here is an imaginary example:*

### The Facts

*My marriage broke up*
*I lost my financial security*
*I lost my teenage children; they left home, disgusted by both of us*
*I lost the security of having a husband*
*I lost the companionship*
*I lost the house I loved*
*I lost my friends through having to move away*
*I lost my Christian status as the wife of a housegroup leader*
*I lost my church, and the new one is horrid*
*I lost my ministry (Sunday School); they don't need me here*

*Both God and Satan want to use this set of circumstances to implement their plans. God wants to use them to bring you good, whereas Satan wants to use them to harm you. So divide the second piece of paper down the middle with a vertical line. At the top of the left side write, 'Satan's Objectives' and on the right side, 'God's Objectives'.*

## Satan's Objectives

*On Satan's side, write down what harm you guess he might hope to achieve. For example:*

> *He wants to make me bitter and angry with my husband for leaving*
> *He wants me to think God is angry with me or doesn't care any longer*
> *He wants to destroy my children's faith and cut them off from us*
> *He wanted to destroy my ministry with the children and house-group*
> *To send me to a church where I am not asked to help in any way*
> *He wants to see me lonely, miserable and bored*

*Your own list will probably be much longer, so do give yourself time to think carefully.*

## God's Objectives

*Look back at your sheet headed 'The Facts' and try to see them from God's angle, then write down on his side of the paper what good he might be wanting to achieve for you. For example:*

> *He wants to help me trust him to meet all my needs*
> *He wants to develop my friendship with him by filling my loneliness with his companionship*
> *He wants to give me a new, warm, forgiving heart*
> *He wants to build my children's faith by my example*
> *He wants me to meet my new neighbours so that I can tell them about him*
> *He wants to use me to bring his reality into this new church*

*Again, don't hurry. You may be amazed at just how long this list can get.*

*When these two battle plans are laid out side by side, it is easier to see just how important we are in the centre of it all. As I said, it is up to us to decide which side wins by how we choose to react. During the whole Broken Teapot Syndrome we may not feel that we control the confusing circumstances, but we* do *control whether they bring good to us and those we love, or whether we let the circumstances destroy us completely.*

# 9

# ANGER

'I've always thought of myself as a reasonably well controlled man; I was punished if I lost my temper as a child. But for two years after I had my stroke, I seemed to boil with anger most of the time. The smallest thing would set me off, and I'd go into these terrible moods when I wanted to lash out at everyone in sight for no apparent reason. Poor old Alice took the brunt of it, and I remember one day, when she was getting ready to go out with one of her irritating girlfriends, she said that she'd left lunch in the microwave. I saw red, and we had the worst row of our married life – she even threatened to leave me.

'Then one evening she asked a colleague from my old firm for dinner. She thought it would cheer me up, but all he did was go on about all the office gossip, and I was so rude in the end that poor Alice didn't know where to put herself. The worst explosion of all happened at church. I'd been feeling upset because things had got so sloppy without me there to keep them on their toes (I'd been administrator for years), but it was the sight of the noticeboard in the church porch that finally did it. I lost my cool, and snapped off the heads of everyone that morning. I felt so ashamed of myself later – getting angry like that was no way for a Christian to behave.'

Tom is not the only Christian to be plagued by anger. It is probably the most dominant emotion in the entire Broken Teapot Syndrome. I am giving it the last place on the list not because it is the least important, but because – for most of us – it seems to be the hardest emotion to handle. Perhaps this is because anger makes us

---

*A fool gives full vent to his anger.* (Prov. 29:11, NIV)

want to hurt someone, and if we cannot get back at the person who caused it all, then we get frightened by the feeling that anyone else will do! Anger makes us react in different ways:

1. *We fight back.* We defend ourselves from further attack by attacking in return, using either our voices to shout, swear and argue, or our bodies to punch, hit, kick or throw crockery. Or we fight back the dignified way, and call in a solicitor to stand up for our rights.

2. *We save it.* We say nothing at the time, but think, 'I'll make him pay for this one day.' While we wait for our chance to get even, we tell everyone we meet how badly he behaved so that they will be angry with him too. We find ourselves hoping that she is unhappy with her admirer, or wonder what would happen if he had a breakdown and lost his job. We might even think how much easier everything would be if he or she were dead.

3. *We divert it* – by venting it on someone else, i.e. shouting at the milkman or kicking the cat when it's really the boss who crossed us.

4. *We turn it inwards.* We hurt ourselves because we dare not hurt others, by inwardly 'shouting' abuse at ourselves, punishing our bodies through excessive physical exertion, reckless driving, nail biting, self-starvation or wild eating binges.

5. *We freeze it* – by turning it into hate: the 'never ever again' kind of ice-cold anger. 'I'll never speak to them again . . . go near him . . . trust her . . . I will never forgive.'

6. *We deny it.* We swallow it down behind a smile that says, 'It doesn't matter, it didn't hurt, of course I'm not angry,' while we lock the anger carefully away in a sealed compartment and pretend it isn't there.

Christians face a dilemma over anger. 'You've got every right to be angry, you can't be a doormat when someone treats you badly,' we are told by the world. 'It's a healthy reaction, and you must let it all come out,' say the experts. But somehow we feel it is 'not done' to bawl and scream abuse at a church meeting, and it isn't scriptural to

---

*Everyone must be quick to listen, but slow to speak and slow to become angry. Man's anger does not achieve God's righteous purpose.* (Jas. 1:19–20, GNB)

give the vicar a black eye. So the 'fight back' method is out, and we opt for methods 2–6 instead – often with disastrous consequences.

Anna had been a minister's wife for twenty years, and keeping the peace between her husband and his flock had taught her to keep her anger under tight control. She was a slim, attractive woman in her early fifties, but she came to see me because she wanted prayer for all kinds of physical symptoms that medical tests could not explain. 'Life's a bit of a mess,' she said wearily. 'Ours was one of the largest Baptist churches in the country. We used to get three hundred regularly on a Sunday morning, but last week there were fifteen people there! It's been such a bad witness, all the gossip and infighting.'

'How did it happen?' I asked.

'Leslie took on an assistant pastor, Trevor – he seemed a super young man, full of spiritual dynamite, and determined to go places in the Christian world. However, it wasn't long before we realised that all he was after was power, and he started stirring people up against Leslie, saying the church was being held back because he was so traditional. When Leslie tried to tell the elders about his misgivings over Trevor, he was accused of being jealous.

'In no time at all, the church was divided down the middle, and it all came to a head when Trevor went off with two-thirds of our membership to start a new fellowship in a school, less than two miles away. Lots of people were so disillusioned that they just stopped going anywhere at all.'

She had told me the story quite calmly, her face expressionless, but something was worrying me.

'You must have felt very angry?' I ventured.

'Angry? Oh no, just sad,' she replied quickly.

'But they hurt you?' She hesitated, apparently struggling with herself as a tinge of red coloured her pale face.

'Well, before the church split up it was a little difficult because Trevor started a rumour that our marriage was breaking up, and that I wanted to control Leslie and dominate the whole church. Then he even spread the word around that my pressurising was making

---

*You are never more vulnerable to sin than when your anger is out of control. Will you use your anger, or let it use you?*
(David Augsburger)

Leslie ill. Because it was only silly gossip, I took no notice. Of course, in the end it was Trevor who made Leslie ill – the whole thing took its toll and he had a terrible breakdown. He nearly died after taking an overdose, and was in the psychiatric hospital for months. That was really the end, because even the people who still came to church began to say it was a sign that God was judging him; and, with no minister, the place soon emptied.'

'How is Leslie now?' I asked.

'He's at home, he potters in the garden – sometimes – but mostly he sits and stares into space. The doctor says he'll probably get better, but his whole personality's changed. He never speaks to me unless he has to, and if he can't snap out of it soon we'll have to leave the manse to make way for a new minister. Goodness only knows where we'll end up then.'

'But how does all this make you react?' I persisted.

'Well, I feel it's my duty to expose Trevor for what he is,' she said grimly. 'A "wolf in sheep's clothing". I've written letters to the powers that be and done my best to open as many eyes as possible. Of course, I can't do much since I became ill myself – that's why I feel I need some prayer.'

'Anna,' I said, when we had asked the Lord how we should pray, 'I feel that anger is causing a lot of your problems.' She looked quite astonished.

'I haven't been angry once throughout all this,' she protested. 'I've learnt to control it.' In reality, she had only learnt to *deny* it. We may think we are behaving like Christians by not losing our tempers, i.e. not letting our anger show, but invisible anger is just as wrong. *We* are supposed to follow the teachings of Christ, and Jesus tells us plainly that *all* anger is bad (when it is sparked by a wrong done to us) (Matt. 5:22).

Obviously Jesus would not approve of the 'fight back' method. He says that when someone hits or insults us we are not to retaliate (Matt. 5:39). The 'save it' method is out, too, because when he talks about anger in Matthew 5:21–24 he does not use the Greek word, *thumos* (a sudden flame that quickly springs up, but just as quickly

---

*Be gentle and ready to forgive; never hold grudges. Remember, the Lord forgave you, so you must forgive others.* (Col. 3:13, LB)

dies down), but uses the word *orge* (long-lived anger that we nurse and brood over). He warns us that 'hell fire' is the consequence of this kind of anger, because it makes us devalue others and he forbids us to plan revenge (v. 39), or to stand up for our rights (v. 40). He also says that what we *think* in our minds is the same as *doing* it. We should hope for good things for our enemy, because wanting nasty things to happen to him or her is as bad as arranging that they will. To imagine killing the person is actually murder!

Jesus would also not approve of the 'divert it' method because he would not want other people to be hurt by our rage. The same applies to the 'turn it inwards' strategy. He loves us, and so does not want us hurt either.

The 'freeze it' reaction in his eyes would be the worst of all, because it denies the possibility of ever forgiving. We have already discussed what that could do to us (see p.44).

So that only leaves us with the 'deny it' option, which most Christians take without realising that this is also condemned in the Bible. 'Get rid of all bitterness, passion, and anger' (Eph. 4:31), and to do so as quickly as possible (Eph. 4:26–27). 'See that no . . . root of resentment, rancour, bitterness or hatred shoot forth and cause trouble and bitter torment and many become contaminated and defiled by it' (Heb. 12:15, AMP).

Jesus does not condemn *all* kinds of anger. He was obviously angry himself on a number of occasions, but always on behalf of others and never because of wrongs done to himself. The Bible tells us, 'in your anger do not sin' (Eph. 4:26, NIV), so there must be times when it is right to *use* anger to lend us the courage to confront bad situations. This is what Jesus did when he demolished an entire livestock market singlehanded, with only a few bits of old rope and lots of righteous indignation. Abraham Lincoln was angry when he saw the slave market in New Orleans, but he used it to give thousands of slaves their freedom. Tolstoy's anger blazed out against war, Gandhi was angry about oppression, and Shaftesbury, Elizabeth Fry and Wilberforce used their anger to confront injustice. Anger comes as a reaction to pain, but for most of us the pain is caused by injuries

---

*And when you stand and pray, forgive anything you may have against anyone, so that your Father in heaven will forgive the wrongs you have done.* (Mark 11:25, GNB)

others inflict on us, and that kind of anger is not the 'Jesus kind'.

## Handling Anger

This wrong kind of anger must be dealt with promptly and efficiently, and here is a formula that I have personally found very helpful. I hope to explain it as this chapter unfolds.

1. Name it
2. Understand it
3. Express it
4. Confess it
5. Explain it
6. Let go of it
7. Use it

Most of us find no. 1 so difficult that we never get any further, and I have learnt from experience just how easy it is to ignore buried anger to the point where it becomes dangerous.

When my mother had a stroke she was already physically frail from serious heart disease. The mental confusion that the stroke caused seemed like a final insult. Our six children were all still tiny, the youngest little more than a baby, but we felt it was right for her to come and live with us. She had to sleep downstairs in our living-room, which did not leave much space in our ordinary 'semi' for the rest of us. In fact, we soon began to feel like rats confined in an overcrowded cage.

Mother used to wake up at three in the morning and demand her breakfast, and if I dashed out to the shops during the day I would discover on my return that she had wandered up the road looking for me, probably in no more than her petticoat; or she'd had an unfortunate accident trying to reach her commode.

Yes, I was angry an awful lot of the time, but I did not realise I was angry because there was no way I could admit it – even to myself. Her constant, unreasonable demands made me feel angry, but it

> *Be kind to each other, tender-hearted, forgiving one another, just as God has forgiven you because you belong to Christ.* (Eph. 4:32, LB)

would have been unthinkable to let her see it because she couldn't help being confused, and it was distressing her enough as it was. Most of my anger came because I loved her and didn't see why God should let her suffer like that, and because my ceaseless efforts to make her happy always ended in failure and frustration. I could not have told Tony how I felt because it would only have made things even worse for him. Everyone else in the world would have said, 'Get her into a home,' but I loved her too much for that. So I felt guilty for being irritable and firmly swallowed my anger.

One morning, when Mother had upset her cup of tea all over her newly changed bed, I suddenly knew I was going to explode – and I had to run out of the room to prevent myself from screaming abuse or even hitting her. I stood in the kitchen, trembling all over with the effort of controlling myself, while trying not to hear her plaintive voice demanding yet another wash and a clean nightie.

I suddenly recognised my anger for what it was and I remembered a foster child called Debbie that we once had. She had a terrible fear of vomiting. When all the other children caught a tummy bug they got rid of it in the usual way and soon felt better. Debbie could not let herself be sick, so the poison remained in her body until she became quite ill. As I stood there in the kitchen I suddenly thought, 'That's what I'm doing to my anger. Holding it all in like this must be bad for me.' Perhaps because I have always found it helpful to think in pictures, I suddenly 'saw' all this swallowed anger going down inside me and being stored in a huge internal tank, like a cesspit situated deep inside me. The thought was so unpleasant that I have never forgotten it.

When someone, for whatever reason, continuously forces down anger over a prolonged period, the anger has to go somewhere. Perhaps we all have one of these underground reservoirs where our unexpressed anger bubbles away undetected and the same old bitter thoughts revolve endlessly in our minds. As more and more fury is pushed down, this underground chamber has to be constantly enlarged to hold the ever-increasing volume.

*The test of forgiveness lies with healing the lingering pains of the past and not with forgetting that the past ever happened.* (Lewis Smedes)

## Naming the Anger

Rumpelstiltskin, that nasty little tyrant in the fairy story, had great power over a princess in distress until the moment he was named. Then he disappeared in a puff of smoke. I think anger is like that. It has such destructive power while we deny its existence, but once we name it for what it is and stop calling it 'hurt feelings' or 'my irritable nature', and once we face the fact that we *are* angry and we have a very valid reason for being angry, there is a chance that Jesus can help us to deal with both the anger and the reason. After all, it would hardly be fair for God to make people with the capacity to be angry, and then condemn most forms of anger, unless he intended to help us manage it correctly – or even learn to use it creatively.

## Understanding the Anger

People who are hurting seem to boil with anger a good deal of the time, as I did while I cared for my mother. We know this huge tank of anger is there, smouldering away under the surface, and silly little things like tea spilt on bedclothes or an untidy church noticeboard spark a flame of irritation that we try hard to smother. We say, 'The spilt tea made me angry', but if we are honest we know these little things are not the real cause. A far bigger lake of frustration lies beneath these trivial pinpricks.

### *When our sources of satisfaction are under threat*

This is what James, the brother of Jesus, says about anger: 'Where do all the fights and quarrels among you come from? . . . You want things, but you cannot have them . . . you strongly desire things, but you cannot get them, so you quarrel and fight' (Jas. 4:1–2, GNB).

> *If a brother sins against you, go to him and show him his fault . . . If he listens to you, you have won your brother back . . . 'Lord, if my brother keeps on sinning against me, how many times do I have to forgive him? Seven times?' 'No, not seven times,' answered Jesus, 'but seventy times seven.'* (Matt 18:15, 21, 22, GNB)

What is it we want so much that we become violently frustrated when we cannot have it? Surely the greatest 'wants' in our lives are to be loved, accepted and needed. The pain when these three crucial needs are not met is so unbearable that we will do anything to find the people or situations that supply them:

1. Being loved makes us feel secure. We find this love first in our parents, then our friends, romantic attachments, spouses and children.
2. Being accepted builds our feeling of worth. This comes through being valued by the people who matter most to us, our family, friends, identity group and workmates. It matters vitally to us to be the kind of person they find attractive, and to live up to their ideals, desires and patterns of behaviour.
3. Being needed makes us feel significant and important as a person. This comes from our work, career, charity activities, clubs, home and possessions, power, positions of leadership, and Christian work or ministry.

When the 'teapot' crashes we may lose the people on whom we depended to give us the love we need, we may no longer be able to do the things that made us feel worth something in our family and community, or we may no longer fill the role or position that made us feel important and significant in our corner of the world.

### Tom's anger

All this causes a feeling of devastation, because we have lost the ways in which we had always met our vital needs. A lot of the fear and depression comes through their loss. The anger comes because the goals we set ourselves in order to achieve this feeling of being loved, accepted and significant are blocked off. All the things we set out to do have been thwarted, and the frustration that results is enormous, but so often we do not know why.

Tom, the man I mentioned at the beginning of this chapter, said, 'I wanted to lash out at everyone in sight for no apparent reason,' but

---

*Our wounds tie us to the past and if we try and forget them, then we keep the past as a jailer over our present. To relive is a commitment to remember and to forgive.* (Russ Parker)

once he realised what the reason was, he reached a turning point. After two years of constant bad temper he went to a Christian counsellor, who helped him to see that all three of his crucial 'life needs' were under attack as a result of his stroke. In spite of the way he treated poor Alice, his greatest fear was that his disability might turn her away from him, because their love had always been the source of all his security. His anger was triggered every time she left him to look after himself, so she could go out with 'her irritating girlfriends'. In his position as a partner in a large firm of London solicitors, people looked up to him — and that made him feel 'he mattered' and had something to contribute to the world. Hearing all the office gossip reminded him that life was going on perfectly normally without him and made him feel as if he no longer counted. His self-worth came through his role as administrator at church. Now he could no longer be the hub of church life he felt devalued and rejected.

Tom emerged from his 'broken teapot' when he found new goals and a different way of meeting his needs – but more about that in the following chapter.

### Anna's anger

It was so easy for me, standing outside the situation, to see that Anna's secret anger was there because Trevor's 'takeover bid' had blocked so many of her life goals. She needed to feel loved by her husband, her security depended on it, but his illness had changed him and he was cold and distant. She needed to feel accepted in order to maintain her self-worth, and being loved and appreciated by a large congregation who had valued her ministry had always provided that. Now she felt most of her friends had rejected her because they believed the lies about her, or left the church just when she needed them most. Her significance in her corner of the world was also under fire, now no one knocked on her door for advice or practical help, and her status in the town as a minister's wife looked

*Paul said, 'I want to know Christ'* (Phil. 3:10, NIV). *To love someone is to long to know him or her even better. And he also said, 'More than anything else . . . we want to please him.'* (2 Cor. 5:9, GNB)

as if it was coming to an end completely. The thought of swapping the status symbol of a lovely big manse for a retirement flat in some strange town where no one knew her felt to her like being 'chucked on the scrap heap'.

Of course, there was also a lot of the right kind of anger too. She was right to be furious when she saw how her husband was suffering so unnecessarily. While Anna insisted she was not angry, though, all these conflicts went on battling inside, completely undetected by her.

It often helps people when they suddenly feel anger surging up inside, and while they are counting up to ten, to ask themselves, 'Which of my needs is being threatened here and what goals are being blocked?'

### Danger! Beware of One of the Greatest Hazards!

To function efficiently, all human beings need to feel loved, accepted and needed, as we have seen, and we look to certain people, activities or roles to satisfy these needs. When our 'teapot' breaks, we often lose these vital sources of satisfaction and we have to search for new ways of meeting our needs. Until we find them, these needs are screaming out to be met – and most of us will do anything to smother the resulting pain. We turn to various things that seem to soothe this pain for a while, but sometimes these very things become 'hold up' factors that prevent us from finding new ways to meet our needs. For instance, certain things such as alcohol, sleeping pills and tranquillisers can be a help at first, but if taken too much for too long they become addictive. Other less obvious things can also be just as habit-forming and destructive: food, nasty videos and magazines, doubtful books and films, casual sex, gambling, or extravagant spending that leads to debt.

Make sure you run for comfort to the 'strong tower' (see p.102), because the Lord says this about people who run in the opposite direction: 'My people have committed two sins: they have turned

---

*One thing I ask of the Lord . . . that I may dwell in the house of the Lord [in his presence, his company] all the days of my life.* (Ps. 27:4, NIV)

away from me, the spring of fresh water, and they have dug cisterns, cracked cisterns that can hold no water at all' (Jer. 2:13, GNB).

## Expressing the Anger

Understanding why we are angry does not help completely, of course: we need to find a safe way of expressing our anger without hurting anyone else. On the day that my mother tipped tea over the bed, I made a firm resolve to have my 'inner tank' drained as soon as possible. I knew I needed to express the anger in some way, but how?

As the mother of a large family, I have always felt it best to allow anger to be legitimate, so long as expressing it does not hurt anyone. Experts may well disagree, but then perhaps they don't have six children! When our second baby was born, Sarah was not yet two. We thought at first that she was delighted with 'her baby', then I began to find her sharp little teeth marks in Justyn's foot or mysterious bumps on his head. Rather than teach her to store her anger or deny it, we went to a jumble sale and bought a large, moth-eaten cuddly toy which became known as Debbie Teddy. It lived in the corner of the playroom, and we explained to Sarah that we understood that she wanted to hurt Justyn, but we couldn't let her because it made him sad; instead she could punch, kick and bite Debbie Teddy, because Teddies never get sad about anything. It worked marvellously for a week or so, and then backfired on us badly because Sarah and Debbie Teddy became so devoted that punching and kicking were out of the question! Yet I cannot remember Sarah ever hurting Justyn again.

As I changed my mother's nightie I considered finding a plump cushion, or knocking up a batch of dough and kneading it violently. I even thought of fetching a hammer and nails from Tony's tool shed and banging out my anger that way. However, I rejected those options: my anger was bigger than that. However, people do find a physical expression helpful such as going for a jog, digging the garden, scrubbing the floor. All those things work well, except for people like Tom in his wheelchair, but he found a substitute in his computer games.

I've always been a 'words person' and therefore I find that expressing anger in that way helps me most. Of course, words can hurt people far more than sticks and stones, so that leaves us with the problem of who to say the words to. It is possibly best not to say them to the person who caused the anger, because the situation may be so volatile that the result could be murder!

There was no one else I could talk out my anger with at that time, and anyway I am sure the very best person to go to is God. In the last chapter we looked at expressing anger towards God himself, but this is something quite different: it is not directing anger *at* God, but pouring it out *before* him.

I had been denying my anger for so long that I felt I wanted to make the expression of it a special occasion, so when a friend said she would take my mother out for the day it gave me an excellent opportunity. Another playgroup Mum said she would keep my two youngest boys for the afternoon and 'give me a real break', so for the first time in years I was quite alone in the house. This was definitely 'clean out day' for those anger tanks. It seemed sensible to get myself into the right mood, so I spent the morning doing all the jobs that make me most bad tempered – and I fasted, too, that day. Eating has not only been one of the ways I have coped with my fears, it has also acted as a lovely, cosy blanket to cover my anger, and I always want to stuff myself with chocolate biscuits when I'm cross. Fasting allows anger to come to the surface, and that's just where I wanted it to be.

By the time my stomach told me it ought to be lunchtime I was almost ready, so I had a bath, washed my hair and put on a clean set of clothes. This was not only because I had cleaned out the chickens and tidied the garage, but because I felt the occasion was so important that I wanted to purify myself as they did in Old Testament times.

Finally, I took the phone off the hook so nothing would disturb me, and locked the back door. Coming into the presence of God is always an awesome thing. In our church we do not go in for visual prompts to worship, such as icons or crucifixes, but that day I felt I needed something to make the whole thing real. So I found a poster that showed two big hands held out as if to a child, and I stuck it on the kitchen wall. The picture helped me to think of God the Father. Then I lit one of the leftover Christmas candles to represent the refining fire of the Holy Spirit. I set the candle on a little table under the picture, and added the cross I had made that morning from two bits of fencing wood. Father, Son and Holy Spirit were all represented, and I was ready at last.

First, I sat down at the table and wrote a long and detailed list of everything that made me angry about life as it was. It took a long time, because it covered several pages, but when it was done I stood in front of the little table and reminded myself just how very great God is. He was there with me, even though I could not see him or feel his presence. Remembering the time when Moses stood before him, I slipped off my shoes. The place where I stood was 'holy ground' (Exod. 3:5). God really would hear what I told him, and I was not just going to express all my anger into empty space. He loved me infinitely, and he cared intensely about how I was feeling.

Then I held the list out to him, and began reading it out loud. I felt such a fool at first, but fortunately, as we lived right out in the country, no one could hear me – if someone had, I might have been certified!

Should you decide to try this way of communicating your anger to God, I am sure that you too will also find it hard to let go of all the filthy, revolting bitterness of your innermost being and to lie there exposed to his sight. It could even be one of the hardest things you have ever had to do. So many of us were brought up in families that denied feelings, and were taught that expressing anger is wrong, so this exercise will be a real psychological hurdle.

Do let yourself feel the strength of your anger as you express it. If you dare, go back to times in the past and stand in your imagination where you stood then, and feel as you felt then. Experience the ferocity of your rage, because unless you are aware of its full power you will never realise its potential danger to yourself and others. Feel it fully as you express it to God. Don't panic halfway through; don't stop to consider just how great and powerful and holy God is. Don't let yourself think how easily he could squash you like an insignificant ant if he chose. He *is* holy, he *is* powerful, he *could* squash you right now, but he also loves you. God has been eagerly waiting for you to throw all this anger at his feet so that he can pick it up and absorb it all for you.

### Confessing the Anger

When my anger was finally expressed and poured out before God, I felt I wanted to kneel and ask him to forgive me for allowing that anger and bitterness to collect down there inside me for so long. All anger (except the Jesus kind) is sin, because it comes when our 'I wants' are not met, so basically it results from selfishness. As I knelt there, I sensed that God was cleaning me out inside, just as I had swept out the garage that morning. All that filthy, rotting anger was gone. It was as if his power was washing out any remaining slime left clinging to the walls of my 'cesspit', scouring them clean, white-washing them, and making everything inside me fresh and new again. The experience was completed when I asked the Holy Spirit of Jesus to come and fill that empty space where all the anger had been, and I felt the warmth of his love flowing into my soul.

Finally, I found the roasting tin we use for turkeys at Christmas and, placing it on the table beside the cross and the candle, I set light to all the sheets of paper and watched my anger writhing and twisting grotesquely as the words disappeared for ever in the refining fire of God's Holy Spirit. The blackened remains went down the kitchen sink, and I just had time to scour the roasting tin thoroughly before my mother was back demanding her tea.

It would be nice to say here that I was never angry again, that I nursed my mother like a perfect saint from that time on. Sadly, that wouldn't be true – perhaps keeping that internal Bitterness Tank free of collected anger has to become a daily job after that initial spring clean. It helped me to understand this when a friend of mine was taken ill in the night while staying with us. She was rushed into hospital for an emergency operation to remove an abscess in her pelvic cavity, and for some time after the surgery a tube was constantly draining away the remaining infection and pus.

During the difficult patches in our lives, when our stress levels are so high that a lot of anger is produced, we do need to keep on expressing and confessing it continuously to the Lord throughout each day, rather like the drip, drip, drip of that drainage tube. If we leave it to collect again for a long period, we will be back in hospital for a further major operation!

## Explaining the Anger

By 'explaining' I mean waiting until we have calmed down, and then telling the person who made us angry how we felt, and, because anger always causes barriers, trying to mend the relationship. We will be looking at practical ways of doing this in Chapter 11, and there is also a section there on how we handle this 'explaining' when the person concerned is dead.

Here, I simply mean, for example, going to the boss and saying,

'Look, I really did find it a bit too much when you gave me all those extra letters to do on a Friday afternoon. Couldn't we sort out a better system next time?' Or saying to the family, 'I'm sorry you're sick of sausages, and I will try and be a bit more creative in future, but it really dents my self-esteem when you criticise my cooking.' That sounds a bit ridiculous, and it certainly wouldn't work in our house, but there is a serious principle behind it.

When Jesus was talking about anger and relationships in Matthew 5:23–24, he tells us to settle our accounts with others very quickly so that they do not escalate and become impossible to pay. In other words, we need to deal correctly with the very first spark of anger, so that it does not become a raging forest fire.

Suppose an imaginary husband remarks mildly that he wishes his wife would grill the sausages rather than always frying them. Her self-esteem is threatened, and a niggle of irritation makes her prod his weak spot: significance. 'If you had a job we could afford steak!' shouts the wife. This produces a small flame of anger, because being unemployed whacks at his need for significance. In turn, he uses the flame to attack just where he knows it will hurt her most, and so it goes on all day, tit for tat, back and forth, and each time a larger amount of anger is generated until a major argument erupts before nightfall.

'I can't think why I ever married you!' is a major attack on security, and soon such huge amounts of anger have been generated that, if left unchecked over a long period, can lead to the kind of raging inferno that divides relationships. Or it could be frozen into the 'I will never ever again' kind of ice-cold hate. There are couples who do not split up, but who stay together for years without ever speaking again.

The Bible says, 'A gentle answer quietens anger' (Prov. 15:1, GNB), and if that first spark of anger over the sausages had been dealt with by a frank explanation or a quick apology it might have changed everything. 'Do not let the sun go down while you are still angry,' says St Paul (Eph. 4:26, NIV): in other words, only carry one day's burden of anger at a time and keep short accounts. 'Let no debt remain outstanding, except the continuing debt to love one another' (Rom. 13:8, NIV).

### Letting the Anger Go

It took Anna a long time to admit she was angry, perhaps because her 'righteous indignation' became confused with the wrong kind of anger.

'Bad situations must be confronted if there is ever to be justice in the world,' she said one evening, as we sat by the fire. 'If Trevor is left unchecked he may do untold damage by his strange ideas. I feel I must take further steps to make people see him for what he really is.'

'Isn't that a bit like taking revenge?' I said it softly, but she heard all right – and for one moment I almost thought she was angry! Instead, she managed to smile as she calmly replied, 'Surely if something is wrong we have a duty to put it right?'

'That is true, but perhaps you are not the right person to do that, seeing that you are emotionally involved?' I suggested.

'If I don't, who else will?' she demanded.

'Couldn't you leave it to God to choose the right person? Surely it is a father's responsibility to deal with a wayward child, and not the responsibility of a sibling, particularly the sibling who has been wronged.'

'God doesn't expect us to be mindless doormats!' Anna said snappily and, looking at her watch, decided it was time she left.

As we met each other regularly, she gradually began to understand just how many of her sources of satisfaction had been threatened by Trevor's actions, and with that understanding came the ability to acknowledge that her anger was there. However, after that point she stuck, excusing herself by saying, 'I can't face up to all this heavy stuff while I'm feeling so ill all the time – and now I'm getting depressed on top of everything else, I just feel I must have space.'

So we talked about other things when she came, until I began to suspect that she was afraid to express and confess her anger in case she would then have to forgive, and her hatred of Trevor was still far too real to allow that.

'Of course I'm willing to forgive Trevor,' she would say suspiciously often, 'but I'm not quite ready to do it yet.' It is hard enough for most of us to admit to anger, but very few will ever acknowledge hate. There was nothing I could do but go on praying for her as the weeks went by.

Then one March weekend, when Anna was staying with her mother who lived close to us, she came round to see me on a Saturday evening. I realised at once that something was different about her, so I asked her directly what it was.

'Well, it only happened this week,' she admitted. 'I've been going to an ecumenical prayer group during Lent, and there's this little old nun who comes along to it. She's such a sweetie. She asked me if I'd like to see the convent where she lives, and I went on Monday afternoon. I had been feeling that something was happening to me inside for a few days,' she added awkwardly. Years of being 'the minister's wife' made it very hard for her to admit any spiritual need of her own. 'I think it's this business about life goals and crucial needs; I think the Lord has been challenging me to trust him to meet *all* my needs, instead of always trying to find ways of meeting my own. Anyway, I told Sister Elizabeth about all that, and she took me into a little oratory off the Convent Chapel, and prayed such a beautiful prayer – asking the Lord to show us what he wanted to do for me.'

Suddenly I noticed that tears were trickling down Anna's thin cheeks. It was the very first time I had ever seen her cry. She went on to explain how the little nun had helped her to express her anger in very much the same way as I had done once. They even burned a long list of all the things that Anna felt that Trevor had taken from her.

'I think it was realising that I could trust God to meet all my needs that finally helped me to get it all out into the open. After we had burnt the papers, that dear old lady even sprinkled me with holy water as a sign that I was cleansed. I dare not think what people would say about me if that got round our Baptist church!' And then I heard her laugh for the first time too! So often, buried anger holds good feelings down as well.

'What about . . . forgiveness?' I asked cautiously, and her smile died away.

'Soon,' she replied, 'but not quite yet.'

Anna and I went to church together the following evening and it was such a special service that Anna spent most of it in tears at the far end of the pew, and I must say I was a bit weepy myself. When it finished, I knew I needed to get to Anna before we were caught up in all the usual chit-chat, so as soon as the other occupants of the pew had left I slid along to sit beside her. She put her head down on my shoulder and wept again.

'I think I've got there at last,' she said.

'Got there?' I asked.

'You know, you nagged me about it often enough. I've reached that place now, but I don't really know what to do now and it scares me a bit.'

So we asked the Lord to show us what he wanted to do for her at that minute, and as we sat there in silence I began to see a picture in my head of a little alpine path, winding up through the fir trees. Anna was trudging up this, struggling under the weight of a very heavy backpack. The path was steep and stony and she often stumbled as she struggled upwards.

Then I saw the path had emerged from the trees on to a stark and rugged mountainside and suddenly I realised it had ended abruptly, leaving the Anna in my picture to stare down into a dark chasm, so deep there seemed to be no bottom to it at all. On the far side, just a few feet away, the path continued, and across the abyss on the far side stood Jesus, his arms held out in welcome.

'Yes, that's exactly how it is!' she said, after I had described the picture to her. 'I've known for months that I would have to decide to trust Jesus completely one day. While I've been fighting for our rights, and trying to sort out our future and prevent Trevor damaging anyone else, I haven't been trusting the Lord to sort it all out. I suppose it's been pride, really, but this evening I kept feeling he was waiting for my decision. It was urgent that I made up my mind one way or the other.'

'How do you feel about that?' I asked, remembering all her questions and prevarications.

'Scared,' she replied, 'because I feel there is something I have to do first, before I leap over that chasm.'

We prayed again, and the picture came back to me very clearly. I saw that if Anna was going to manage that leap across the chasm, she would have to take off her backpack and leave it behind.

'What do you think is inside it?' I asked her.

She frowned in her effort to get into the picture with me.

'Perhaps it's my props,' she suggested, 'the things I always used to think were so important in my old life.'

'Is there anything deeper down in the bag?' I asked her, and she flushed.

'Yes, but I don't want to look at them.' The struggle took Anna a long time, and she was silent for what seemed to me like hours. Finally she looked at me and said, 'Jen, they're all the grudges I've been carrying against Trevor and the other people who left the church and said such terrible things about Leslie and me. I think,' she added with a sob, 'there's a lot of hatred in that bag too.'

'Are you going to be able to leave the bag behind you when you leap that chasm?' I asked. Again she was silent for a very long time.

'I want to,' she said slowly, 'but I just don't see how it's possible to forgive someone who did such a lot of damage.'

'I think Jesus is saying, "try it",' I said gently.

'I can't!' she said, suddenly drawing away from me. 'It's too hard, why should God expect me to forgive them on top of everything else he's asking of me these days?'

'Try it, Anna,' I said again.

'He'll have to lift me across the chasm then,' she said morosely.

'He can't,' I said. 'You've got to take that backpack off and make the decision yourself to jump. No one can help you with that. Once you are over on the far side, *then* he'll help you with the "how to" part of forgiving.'

Anna finally made that leap of faith with many tears shed on my shoulder. I can never wear that orange blouse without remembering the great sodden patch she left behind on it as she made her quantum leap. At last she looked up at me, with red, swollen eyes, but a radiant smile.

'I've never seen one of your "pictures" before,' she said, 'but I just saw myself in his arms. Saw them tight round me and I realised the utter safety of my position in life now. I am truly *in* Christ. He is my sufficiency. I've just told him, "I shall love you whatever you do, or don't do. I shall love you whether you make things easy for me or not. I shall love you because you are all that matters to me in the world now." Why, oh why, has it taken me so long to reach this lovely place?' Then she added, 'It's not enough to be willing to forgive – one day you have to make that leap and decide to do it.'

## The 'Hold Up' Factor

Anna was profoundly right. That is what the 'hold up' factor is all about in the anger stage: refusing to forgive the person who broke the teapot.

Many people walk all the way through the stages we have described and right up the mountain path, but when they reach the chasm, they stop, look inside their backpacks, and decide they cannot leave those grudges behind. So they put them back inside again, and struggle off down the mountain with the heavy bag still

on their shoulders. These people never come out of the Broken
Teapot Syndrome.


## The Challenge: Using the Anger

God's kind of anger rages furiously on behalf of someone he loves.
When we use the wrong kind of anger to defend ourselves and to
right our own wrongs, God leaves us to it, but when we turn to him
and leave him to put matters right in his own way and at his own
time, he is committed to helping us. 'Do not take revenge, my friends,
but leave room for God's wrath, for it is written: "It is mine to avenge;
I will repay," says the Lord' (Rom. 12:19, NIV).

Our wrong kind of anger gets in the way of God's right kind of
anger because, 'The Lord will fight for you, and there is no need for
you to do anything' (Exod. 14:14, GNB).

Perhaps these are the questions that the Lord wants to ask in this
challenge:

• 'Will you let me sort all this out for you?'
• 'Will you let me use your righteous anger to help me defend the
  other people I love?'

Once Anna had shifted all her hatred out of the way, she was able
to see who her real enemy was – Satan, not Trevor. Satan had
organised the whole thing, and Anna could be justly angry at what
he had done to Leslie and the faith of many younger Christians. So
she used that anger to 'do something about it' by going into
spiritual warfare through prayer. She felt so much better physically
that she found that she could get up early in the mornings for a real
time of intercession before her husband woke. She prayed for his
health and the broken body of the church, and she prayed for
Trevor too. She realised that when Jesus said, 'Behold, I stand at the
door, and knock: if any man hear my voice, and open the door, I will
come in to him' (Rev. 3:20, AV), he was speaking to a whole church,
not simply to an individual. It only takes one person to open the
door of a church, a family or any other situation, and to allow the
mending power of Jesus to come into the centre of all the pain and
hurt.

Anna then gathered some of the women who were still left in the
congregation, and with newfound enthusiasm and energy she
encouraged them to begin praying with her for the healing of the

church. They fasted each Monday and met together in twos and threes at other times of the week.

As Leslie began to improve in health and the life of the church started to move on again, many of the 'scattered sheep' returned to the fold and once more numbers began to grow. In the end, it was Anna who helped both churches to patch up their differences – and today both fellowships are flourishing side by side, one catering more for the needs of younger people, and the original church for older Christians and those with more traditional tastes. A messy situation has been turned into an opportunity for growth, because one apparently defeated woman used the anger she had always denied to give her courage to fight a battle with spiritual weapons.

---

## A Meditation

King David was one of the fiercest fighters of all time, but he was also known as 'a man after God's own heart'. The anger that sent him out to fight Philistines was God's kind of anger; it burned on behalf of his people who were being attacked without mercy.

One afternoon, when he was a very old man, David sat in a shady corner of his palace courtyard, drowsily remembering. His fighting days were over now, but he was living his greatest battles all over again. Then suddenly a dark memory came back to him and he stirred restlessly on his couch. The wind was moaning among the lonely caves of the desert, where he was hiding like a fugitive in danger of his life.

He had been banished from his position at court with his reputation in tatters, stripped unjustly of all he had in the world, and divided from his best friend for ever. It was all because of the jealousy and hatred of King Saul, who was out there in the darkness, hunting him relentlessly like some animal. But he could so easily have killed his enemy during that dark night that he was remembering now. He had discovered him lying alone and defenceless at the mouth of a cave. A sharp spear was in David's hand – should he plunge it into Saul's black heart and end his own problems for ever? After all, God had said that he should be king some day, so perhaps this was the way it was 'meant'. However, David had turned away, and left Saul to God's anger and vengeance.

He woke with a start, almost expecting to find himself still in the desert, but the beauty of his palace surrounded him. God's anger had burned on his behalf, and Saul had long since gone. But the shadow of another enemy had darkened his life since then, and sadly the old man bowed his head as he remembered another terrible day. This memory was more recent, and he saw himself already frail and bent with age. This time it was not jealousy and hatred that was driving him away from all he valued, but the greed of a young man who wanted his crown – his own son Absalom, the son he loved so much he would willingly have died for him.

David, who had always been admired for his bravery, looked like a coward the day he ran away from his city fortress and left it waiting for Absalom. As he trudged away he was cursed and publicly insulted by one of his son's supporters.

'Your majesty, let me go and cut off his head!' said one of David's men as the old king was pelted with stones. But David shook his head and said simply, 'It may be that the Lord will see my distress and repay me with good for the cursing I am receiving today.'

That is how it had happened in the end, and once again it was God's anger and not David's that came to his defence. As David sat there in the evening of his life, he wrote his final Psalm as a tribute to the powerful but terrible anger of God Almighty.

'My God is my protection, and with him I am safe . . . In my trouble I called to the Lord . . . In his temple he heard my voice . . . Then the earth trembled and shook . . . because God was angry. Smoke poured out of his nostrils . . . He tore the sky apart and came down . . . flashes of fire came from the lightning . . . when you rebuked your enemies, Lord, and roared at them in anger. The Lord reached down from above and took hold of me . . . he rescued me from my powerful enemies and from all those who hate me . . . When I was in trouble . . . the Lord protected me.' (Selected verses from Psalm 18, GNB.)

## A Prayer

*'Come to me all you who are tired of being hurt over and over again, for "I offered my back to those who beat me, my cheeks to those who pulled out my beard; I did not hide my face from mocking and spitting".'* (Isa. 50:6, NIV)

Lord, it's all very well to say I must forgive – it would be easy if everything was all over and done with and safely in the past. But my enemy keeps on hurting me, rejecting me, heaping pain on top of pain, and so many insults that I do not know how to endure it sometimes. I decide to forgive and then bang! He hits me again. I struggle up to my feet and bang! Down I go. Bang! Another humiliation. Bang! Something else is taken away. Bang! Bang! Bang! Over and over again. This repeated pain is driving me mad; how can I possibly forgive something like this that goes on and on? Bang! Bang! Bang! Yet you did.

I suppose it wasn't *afterwards* that you forgave; you did not wait until you could look back on your enemies and see them in retrospect; it was while they were hammering in those nails . . . Bang! bang! Bang! . . . that you said, 'Father, forgive them, they don't know what they are doing.' Each of those nail blows into your hands was rejecting all the loving things those hands had done for mankind. They were the very hands that had formed and created those soldiers; they had hidden the iron in the earth out of which the nails were forged. Bang! Bang! Bang! They rejected you, insulted and humiliated you as well, as they hit you over and over again. Yet you still forgave. Oh Jesus, forgive me for not forgiving too.

Lord Jesus, help me to see what it really means to have you living in me. You feel through my emotions, hurt in my body; these things that they do to me, they do to you too. You say, 'The insults that are hurled at you have fallen on me.' Lord, when they smash my life, they smash your life too. When they insult me, they insult you in me. When they steal my reputation and good name, they steal your honour too. I know you feel angry for me and will fight on my behalf. Help me to rest in that fact.

I am glad I can leave you to be angry with them for me, for your anger is so much more terrible than mine could ever be. I *want* your wrath to burn with vengeance until they are punished in full. Yet as you prayed, 'Father, forgive them', you were asking that they should be let off that punishment, pleading that the terrible wrath of God should *not* wreak vengeance on them. Those men will stand next to me in your presence for all eternity as free and as loved as I am. Lord, please give me the same supernatural forgiving grace – help me love my enemy as you loved yours.

## STOP FOR A MOMENT

### Why Is Forgiving So Hard?

#### 1. It Is Unnatural

*No one expects a rabbit to forgive the fox who has just half eaten it. The natural world says 'an eye for an eye' and 'every man for himself', but as followers of Christ we are told not to conform to the standards of this world; instead, 'let God transform you inwardly by a complete change of your mind' (Rom. 12:2, GNB).*

#### 2. It Is Unpopular

*After a two-year-old called Jamie was brutally beaten to death by two older boys, a clergyman suggested in his pulpit that the only way for anyone to cope with such an atrocity is by forgiveness. Immediately, five members of the congregation stormed out of the church. After some outrageous tragedy, some people regard forgiving as weak, soft or downright wrong. A friend of ours, a clergyman in Dover, spent weeks helping grieving relatives after the Zeebrugge ferry disaster. In his address at the memorial service, which was conducted at sea over the place where the ferry went down, he said that only forgiveness could mend broken lives. His words stirred up a hornets' nest of rage from the media.*

*When I went to speak at Enniskillen in Northern Ireland, I met friends and family members of those killed or hurt in the bomb blast there on Remembrance Day 1987. I told them how much it had helped the rest of us to hear how they stated their willingness to forgive so publicly, but was told that the harsh criticism they had received from people who felt they had no right to forgive such evil had caused them almost as much suffering as the tragedy itself.*

#### 3. It Takes So Long

*Forgiveness is not a once-won battle, but a lifelong war. Just before he died, C. S. Lewis wrote to his American friend Mary: 'Do you know, only a few weeks ago I realised suddenly that I had at last forgiven the cruel school master who so darkened my childhood. I'd been trying to do it for years; each time I thought I'd done it, I found after a week or so it all had to be attempted over again.' Many people give up and feel they have failed simply because they think forgiveness should be as instant as coffee or packet mashed potato. Forgiving is a lengthy process, and it can be the hardest thing Jesus ever asks us to do for him; yet nothing gives him more pleasure than when we make the attempt to forgive. Surely this must be because forgiving was the reason he came to our world in the first place. It cost him everything he had to make forgiveness possible, so perhaps it is no wonder that we find it so costly.*

# 10

# ACCEPTANCE

So what is the 'last square' on the game board of adjustment and change – this mysterious 'state' the experts call acceptance? Could it be the moment when we turn away from the empty display cabinet where the old teapot used to stand and catch our first glance of the new teapot on the windowsill? The time when we realise that we are no longer in tragic pieces scattered all over the kitchen floor, but beautiful in a new kind of way as fresh green shoots push their way out of all the cracks, gaps and broken places.

And how do we know when we reach this 'mysterious moment'? On the day I was thinking out this chapter, a curious thing happened. It was one of those beautiful November days, when a rather elderly sun was painting the remaining autumn leaves in quite impossible colours. So I went for a long walk up my favourite valley near Alfriston in Sussex.

The Cuckmere River winds in elegant ox-bow curves between the flinty chalk hills that eventually become the Seven Sisters – this particular river has always fascinated me because it alters its character completely with the changing tides. Sometimes it is nothing more than a little stream bubbling over the stones at the bottom of deep muddy banks. When the tide is in, however, the level

---

*I will sprinkle clean water on you and make you clean from all your idols and everything else that has defiled you. I will give you a new heart and a new mind . . . I will put my spirit in you and I will see to it that you follow my laws . . . I will save you from everything that defiles you. (Ezek. 36:25–29, GNB)*

of the water rises right to the top of the banks, creating a wide smooth surface on which the swans glide gracefully.

That day, as I walked up the valley, the tide came in after me, and by the time I reached the little bridge at Littlington it was fuller than I had ever seen it before. I noticed it as I paused on the bridge. It was easy to see that the tide was still racing in at high speed because a great sheet of scum, froth and bubbles came racing towards me from the direction of the sea, carrying with it all kinds of straw, twigs and driftwood.

The water was so high that it was not far below the level of the bridge, and as I stood there looking down I thought anxiously, 'If the tide doesn't turn soon, the river is going to burst its banks and flood the cottages in the village.' Then just as the blanket of scum was right under the bridge beneath me, it suddenly slowed down and stopped – and I mean suddenly. It was as if someone had put on the brakes; there was nothing gradual about it. For a moment the water in the river was motionless; it neither flowed in nor out, then a few foamy bubbles from one corner of the slick detached themselves and began to move back slowly downstream. Within seconds, the whole mass followed, and was soon hurrying back towards the sea, from whence it had come. The tide had turned.

I have never seen it actually happen before; usually you only know the tide must have turned because rocks or posts begin to appear that were submerged half-an-hour before. Yet there must always be a moment in time when the tide does turn, whether we happen to perceive it or not. For some people, the Broken Teapot Syndrome seems to get worse and worse as it builds up to a crescendo of misery – just like a floodtide that threatens to burst the banks of their endurance and plunge them into total disaster. Then an event such as a new job, or moving house, or a sudden revelation like Anna's 'alpine leap' or my 'baptism' in cow dung, changes everything so suddenly that they can pinpoint the exact moment when the tide of their affairs actually turned. For others, things improve slowly and imperceptibly so that acceptance feels more like a gentle receding of pain, and a gradual awakening to a new life. Yet even for them, there must have been 'a moment' when the tide turned, even though they were not aware of it at the time.

---

*We will reap a harvest of blessing if we don't get discouraged and give up.* (Gal. 6:9, LB)

This is the stage the textbooks call 'acceptance', but I am not sure I like that word. It conjures up in so many people's minds a sigh of resignation, a surrender to defeat, or a bowing down to an inevitable fate. Real acceptance is not like that at all. In *Beyond Ourselves* (Hodder & Stoughton), Catherine Marshall writes, 'Resignation is barren of faith in the love of God . . . Resignation lies down quietly in the dust of a universe from which God seems to have fled, and the door of Hope swings shut.' Acceptance is a deliberate decision to let go of the past, to step away from the person we were and to move into the future. Boldly embracing it rather than shrinking away. Acceptance is a strong word, a life giving experience.

But surely many people successfully reach this place of acceptance without any Christian faith – if it is only a matter of letting go of the past and deciding to step into a new future. Yet acceptance, for Christians, is also something more, because God is involved in the process.

The issue for a Christian is:

1. Now that the past lies behind me, do I still trust God in spite of all that has happened?
2. Now that the future lies ahead of me, do I trust God to be there in it with me and take care of all my needs?

Nowadays, I am beginning to prefer the word 'abandonment'. Acceptance is something you do through your mind, but abandonment has to be done through the heart.

### What Does It Mean to Abandon Ourselves to God?

Strange as it may sound, it was in Marks & Spencer's that I first realised what the word 'abandonment' really means!

Just before Christmas last year, I was in the store looking for a chunky jumper as a present for Sarah's husband, Paul. Among the

> *God who began the good work within you will keep right on helping you grow in his grace until his task within you is finally finished on that day when Jesus Christ returns.* (Phil. 1:6, LB)

crowds I noticed a little boy of about three, tightly holding on to his father's hand. His eyes were big and round with the wonder of the occasion, which his father was making particularly special for him. They were obviously there to buy a Christmas present for an older sister.

'You see, I wanted her to have slippers with cats' heads on them and *real* whiskers,' he explained earnestly to the startled girl at the check-out desk, as he handed her the pair he had chosen.

'Come on, David,' said his father, and I watched him walk away proudly carrying his green carrier bag.

A while later, when I was queueing up to pay for Paul's jumper, I saw a very different David indeed. He was running frantically through the shop, diving this way and that, round the high counters and displays. He had obviously lost his father, and my instinct was to run up to him and take his hand.

Sadly, children these days have to be warned not to trust strangers, and I decided that he might have become even more frightened if I had approached him. So instead I prayed for him as I wrote out my cheque. Then, with my own green carrier bag in my hand, I went to see if he was all right. In the far distance I caught sight of him standing rigid in the centre of an aisle, his face puce with anger. His precious shopping bag lay on the ground where he had flung it in his baffled fury. He had obviously searched the shop frantically, and had now decided that he had been abandoned for ever and would never be found again. Fear, anger, doubt and utter despair flitted across his face as he stood there, immobilised by his emotions.

This time, I really felt I must take action, but someone else reached him first. She was an elderly lady with thick glasses and bristly warts all over her chin. 'Come along, sonny,' she said, as she grabbed his arm. She meant well, but David shrank away in sheer terror.

Sometimes, when you have run in all directions looking for your security, there comes a moment when there is nowhere left to run; David seemed to have reached that point, so he simply pulled the plug out on the world and collapsed into a heap on the floor. He did not cry, because there is also a place beyond tears and it seemed that

---

**Man's chief end is to glorify God and enjoy him for ever.**
(Westminster Catechism)

he had reached that place. He curled himself into a ball – a defenceless little hedgehog without any prickles. It was then, much to my relief, that I saw David's father appear around the end of the counter.

'David!' he called. What a transformation! The little boy sprang to his feet and ran with quite remarkable speed towards his father. I held my breath, for sometimes when parents find a lost child they lambast them – hard – for being so naughty. I felt as if I couldn't bear that to happen to David, but this father was different. He squatted down to David's level and held out his arms – wide, and David ran straight into them to be lifted high off the ground; his little legs swinging free, in utter abandonment to his father's love.*

### 1. Abandonment Means Trusting God
### for Everything that Lies Behind Us

Look before you leap! Take a positive look at the past!

One of the most painful results of loss is that so many of the goals we used to aim for in life suddenly become impossible to achieve. Perhaps, for example:

- You always wanted to have a happy Christian family. So when your teenagers get mixed up with drugs and bad company, or your spouse wants a divorce, you feel devastated.
- You always wanted to provide for the people you love, but your bankruptcy and endless unsuccessful job applications make you feel a failure.
- You always wanted to be a vet (or a dancer or whatever), so that

---

* Does that story make you cringe because you think that if that is what abandonment to God is all about, you don't feel it's for you? Do you sometimes find it a bit difficult to trust God completely and feel really comfortable with him? Perhaps you should look back again to page 143 and check that you have not developed a wrong picture of what God is like through contact with people in the past. If you ask God to correct any wrong concepts you have, he most certainly will.

---

*And when we obey him, every path he guides us on is fragrant with his loving-kindness and his truth.* (Ps. 25:10, LB)

you felt your life was shattered when the accident resulted in you being in a wheelchair.
- You always wanted to serve the Lord by helping other people, building up your church fellowship, developing a powerful ministry, leading others into the faith, running the youth work housegroup or Sunday School. So when others no longer wanted you or your health broke down, you felt that your life had no purpose.

One of the positive things about the Broken Teapot Syndrome is the opportunity it gives us to consider if such life goals were the right ones in the first place:

- Perhaps the goals we used to think were so important were all good things, but had become *too* important to us. Had they begun to rule our hearts to the point where our lives mean nothing now we cannot achieve them?
- If the things we so badly wanted could be lost as easily as this, were they wise goals to be aiming for anyway? Surely we would be more fulfilled if we aimed at goals that we could be sure of achieving, whatever happens to us in the future.
- Had we managed to achieve those old goals, would they actually have brought us the fulfilment we hope they would have brought us?
- Our previous goals may have been good ones, but were they the goals God wanted for us?

### 2. Abandonment Means Being Willing to Change Our Goals for the Future

What does God think is the most important thing in life? Jesus was once asked that question by a crafty lawyer, but the question was couched in the theological language of his day.

'Teacher, what is the first and greatest commandment?' he asked.

---

*Oh Lord, I know it is not within the power of man to map his life and plan his course . . . Show me the path where I should go, O Lord; point out the right road for me to walk.* (Jer. 10:23 and Ps. 25:4, LB)

Jesus replied promptly in the following vein, 'Loving God with everything you have. All your affections and willpower, with all your physical strength and mental capacity, through your emotions and entire personality. It is our relationship with God that is the most important thing in life, and after that our relationship with other people.'

In other words, there is nothing more important in life than to please God, know him, love him, spend time with him, and make him our treasure and heart's desire. Our goal in life needs to be *him* – not just serving him, or pointing others to him, or doing good, or turning the world upside down. It is not wanting to receive power or spiritual gifts from him, but just wanting *him* for his own sake.

When we want to please God and make him happy every minute of the day, that may mean serving him in all the ways listed above – or perhaps none of them ever again – but when we really want to please him we are willing to leave it to him to decide what he does with us.

This passionate single-minded pursuit of God himself is a goal that is not thwarted by being in a wheelchair or by being kicked out of your church, left to live alone, or robbed of a ministry by the lies and insults of others. It is not affected by any earthly loss, and nothing from heaven will ever thwart it because this is God's goal for us too.

Jesus said, 'Do not store up riches for yourselves here on earth, where moths and rust destroy, and robbers break in and steal. Instead, store up riches for yourselves in heaven . . . For your heart will always be where your riches are' (Matt. 6:19–21, GNB). 'Let Almighty God be your gold, and let him be silver, piled high for you. Then you will always trust in God and find that he is the source of your joy' (Job 22:25–26, GNB).

One of the greatest achievers in history was St Paul. He travelled all over the Roman world making converts and founding churches. When his 'teapot' broke and he was confined to a prison cell, he obviously had time to review his goals and consider what he most wanted out of life.

---

*Happy is the person who remains faithful under trials, because when he succeeds in passing such a test, he will receive as his reward the life which God has promised to those who love him.* (Jas. 1:12, GNB)

'All I want is to know Christ . . . and become like him' (Phil. 3:10, GNB), he said from his prison. That was a goal that was not blocked when he lost his freedom, but had his desire been to change the world he would probably have died of frustration. Was he able to say he had found the secret of contentment (Phil. 4:12) because his goal was the highest one of all, and the only goal that can be achieved by anyone, at any time, in any circumstances?

But how can we 'know Christ'? The idea that suffering brings us closer to Christ is not a popular one these days, but I have seen it happen for so many people that I cannot possibly doubt the truth of it. Many of us can say with Job as he looked back on his terrible experience of suffering, in the past 'I knew only what others had told me, but now I have seen you with my own eyes' (Job 42:5, GNB).

When Paul told us his goal was to 'know Christ', he also explains how that goal can be achieved. The full version of what he said from his dismal prison cell and under sentence of death was this, 'I want to know Christ and the power of his resurrection and the fellowship of sharing in his sufferings, becoming like him in his death' (Phil. 3.10, NIV). Paul had known that 'resurrecting power' once before when he had been in prison; it had been strong enough to burst the Roman fortress apart by an earthquake, setting him free instantly (Acts 16). However, he is telling us that we do not only get to know someone by sharing with them the highest and happiest moments of their lives, but also by sharing with them their deepest and most painful feelings, thoughts and experiences. Through the little prayers at the end of each chapter we have tried to identify with Jesus in his difficult moments as we gave him our own painful feelings and thoughts. It is a habit well worth acquiring.

### 3. Abandonment Means Feeling Safe Right Now in the Present

When little David ran into his father's arms, he felt safe. He knew that his father would, and could, meet all his needs. When Jesus said, 'Happy are those who long to be just and good, for they shall be completely satisfied' (Matt. 5:6, LB), surely when he said 'completely satisfied' he meant that God will meet in full our crucial need for love, acceptance and significance. 'Come, everyone who is thirsty . . . Come . . . buy corn . . . Come! Buy wine and milk – it will cost you nothing! Why spend money on what does not satisfy? Why spend your wages and still be hungry? . . . Come to me, and you will have life!' (Isa. 55:1–3, GNB).

## The challenge

### Can God give us all the security we need?

● Can he love us with unearned, unending, uncondemning, unchanging love, which is so enormous it couldn't possibly get any bigger?

### Can God give us back our self esteem?

● Can he accept us individually for what we are here and now, this very minute, regardless of what we do or fail to do, and accept us so completely that our sense of worth and personal value is complete?

### Can God make life worth living?

● Can God's enjoyment of our company and desire to work in partnership with us provide us with all the significance and importance that we need? That is what we have to decide before we make that leap of abandonment.

### Perhaps God might ask us:

● Why have you always looked to people to meet your crucial needs?
● Why are you always hunting for love and security from human beings? They will always fail you in the end, perhaps not deliberately, but death or illness may prevent them from being there when you need them most. But I love you – I will never leave you or forsake you.
● Why have you always wanted people to like you in order to feel accepted and worth something? Why are you always trying to please, to do and say the things that will make the 'right people' approve of you? Why do you always strive to be the person they want you to be? Why worry about the opinions of people, when

humans only affect you in this life? Why don't you care what I think of you when I have your eternal destiny in my power? (Matt. 10:28.) You will never please people consistently enough to give you the affirmation you need. But to me, you will always be precious.

- Why do you look to your church activities, your job or role in the home to make you feel needed and significant as a person? People are so changeable that one moment you are their superstar and the next a mere nothing. Why look to them to make you feel that your life counts for something? When you are dead and gone, what will earthly importance matter anyway? It is your relationship with me that will last for ever. 'What good will it be for a man if he gains the whole world, yet forfeits his soul?' (Matt. 16:26, NIV.) Remember, I honour you, to me you are important. 'I will condemn the person who turns away from me and puts his trust in man . . . but I will bless the person who puts his trust in me. He is like a tree growing near a stream . . . not afraid when hot weather comes, because its leaves stay green; it has no worries when there is no rain; it keeps on bearing fruit' (Jer. 17:5–8, GNB).

God says to us: 'You are precious and honoured in my sight, and . . . I love you' (Isa. 43:4, NIV). In this verse God promises in just one sentence to be the three things we need!

- He says we are loved – that is our security
- He says we are precious – that is our self-worth
- He says we are honoured – that gives us significance

During a lifetime we will probably love quite a number of people, but very few will be really precious to us, but how many people can we honestly say we *honour*? That means esteeming them very highly, taking careful note of their opinions, and attaching great importance to all they say and do. God not only loves us, but he *honours* us too! And that has to be true – because he would have to honour someone extremely highly before being willing to die for them.

So we are absolutely loved, invaluably precious and highly honoured, both now and in the next life – what more could we want?


## 4. Abandonment Means Being Willing for a New Identity

The fear of changing into something new has been the 'hold up' factor for many people, but this last stage of abandonment entails a willingness to accept life as the new 'teapot' God has been designing all this time. Three little things might still be bothering people about the thought of that:

● 'If I depend on God for everything, does that mean I'll have to live alone for ever, with just him for company?'

There may be all kinds of things we want in the new life ahead – a husband, children, new friends, good relationships at work. When we begin to look to God to be the source of all our needs, it does not mean that he will force us to live like a hermit in the wilderness so that he himself can meet all our needs without human assistance. When God wanted to meet the needs of his first friend, Adam, he met them by sending another human being, Eve, to do it for him: 'It is not good for the man to be alone' (Gen. 2:18, NIV). As I have already said earlier in this book, we can always trust God to send along human arms to 'cuddle sad people' when he knows it is arms and a cuddle that we need. However, we do have to remember that God can see our *needs*, but we can only see our *wants*. Only he knows the difference!

● 'Surely it can't be right for God to want us all to spend our lives worshipping him and "sitting at his feet" in contemplation, like Mary of Bethany. He *must* want a few Marthas around to get things done.'

St Teresa of Avila once said, 'Our Lord is best served by a blend of both Mary and Martha', and of course making our personal relationship of love with the Lord our top priority does not mean that he will never ask us to serve him in more practical ways.

Jesus met a man once who was at the height of one of the most terrible Broken Teapot Syndromes of all time. His name was Legion. He had once been an ordinary family man, with a job and a little house in Decapolis. We don't know what went wrong for him, but gradually he began to open himself up to evil until finally he committed himself to Satan entirely, and many demons were sent to invade his life and possess him completely. Terrible anger burned in him, and would burst out at people uncontrollably until he became so dangerous that they threw him out of the community and chained him among the rocks and graves of the dead. His anger had no outlet then, so he turned it on himself as he mutilated his body, cutting and slashing at it with anything sharp he could find. The evil spirits tormented him until he was too afraid to sleep at night; sometimes, panic lent him such enormous strength that he burst the chains that fettered him and he wandered through the hills in the darkness, alone in his terrible isolation and despair. Then one morning at dawn, Jesus walked up the beach towards him.

It only took a moment to set Legion free from the evil spirits and all the anger, fear and despair they had caused, and his broken life was changed into something astonishingly different. When the local farmers came to complain to Jesus about the loss of their pigs, they were stunned when they saw Legion. Here was the man they had feared and despised, sitting beside Jesus, laughing and talking quite normally. It had been years since they had seen him washed, shaved and wearing clothes. 'When anyone is joined to Christ, he is a new being; the old is gone, the new has come' (2 Cor. 5:17, GNB).

The farmers found the whole thing so unnerving that they ordered Jesus to leave at once, without giving him a chance to tell the people of the ten little towns in that district that he had also come to set *them* free – not just Legion. 'Clear off!' they shouted menacingly.

Legion wanted to go with Jesus, to spend the rest of his life with him, 'sitting at his feet and hearing his words', but Jesus knew Legion was his only hope of reaching those towns. Mark 5:18–20 (GNB) says: 'As Jesus was getting into the boat, the man . . . begged him, "Let me go with you!" But Jesus would not let him. Instead, he told him, "Go back home to your family and tell them how much the Lord has done for you and how kind he has been to you." So the man left and went all through the Ten Towns, telling what Jesus had done for him. And all who heard it were amazed.' Mark also tells us how well Legion did his job of spreading the message (Mark 6:53–56). When Jesus went back some time later, the people were all waiting for him, and they 'ran throughout the whole region' gathering together all the other 'broken teapots' for him to mend.

It is a 'changed life' that convinces people more than anything else that Jesus can also help them. One day when they ask you, 'However did you manage to get through that awful experience?', you will be able to tell them 'how much the Lord has done for you and how kind he has been to you'; and it might be your personal testimony that will introduce *them* to him too.

● 'But how do I know what God really wants to do with me in the future?'

It infuriates most of us to have so few of our questions answered, but we are left in no doubt over this one. Like most other fathers, who want their children to 'take after them', God's goal for our lives is to make us like himself. He has always wanted that, since the beginning of time when he said, 'let us make man . . . in our likeness' (Gen. 1:26, NIV). Yet we never knew quite what God was really like until he sent Jesus down to earth to show us. God wants us to take a good look at Jesus and then to become like him.

### *But what does that mean?*

It simply means living in the ordinary circumstances of our lives as Jesus would. Trying to treat the people in our world as he would treat them, looking at them through his eyes, thinking about them as he does, reacting to them as he would and relating to them in the way he might have done when he had a physical body and lived on earth.

Paul says, 'those whom God had already chosen he also set apart to become like his Son' (Rom. 8:29, GNB), and we 'are being transformed into his likeness with ever-increasing glory' (2 Cor. 3:18, NIV).

### *But I could never do it!*

Well, God certainly does not stand at a distance and shout, 'You've got to change and become like my Son, so start working at it right now!' That would burden us with a crushing load of 'oughts' and 'shoulds' just when we feel too weak to carry anything extra at all. And however hard we tried, there is no way in a billion years we could possibly change ourselves to become like him. Instead, God uses exactly the same method as I explained on p. 27. The diagram there shows that when we ask him to come into the centre of our lives, he fills us up completely with himself. Jesus comes into our lives by his Spirit (John 20:22), and as we make more and more room for him, so he is able to change us from the inside until the difference also begins to show on the outside. He gives us a totally new heart to be the seat of our will and affections (Ezek. 36:26); he gives us his mind to think with (Rom. 12:2), and he helps us to develop his personality and attributes (Gal. 5:22). That is the secret of how we become Jesus 'look-a-likes'.

### 5. Abandonment Means Contentment –
### 'In Acceptance Lieth Peace'*

Being a mended 'teapot' may mean a wonderful, exciting new life, far better than the old one ever was, but it could just as easily mean we still have to live alone, remain trapped inside a painful or disabled body; or we may have to go on sharing our lives with difficult, unkind people who misunderstand us and reject our love. We may never get another job or develop a new ministry; we might have very little money and very few friends. Yet we know that all these things are not the sources of our real satisfaction, and we can say with the Psalmist, 'What else have I in heaven but you? since I have you, what else could I want on earth? My mind and my body may grow weak, but God is my strength; he is all I ever need' (Ps. 73:25–26, GNB). That was the verse that came to me that day by the sea in Devon when I 'felt' Jesus was saying, 'All you need is me.'

It was identifying with Jesus at a deep level that made it possible for Paul to say he was completely happy, even though he was confined in that prison cell under sentence of death: 'For to me, to live is Christ and to die is gain' (Phil. 1.21, NIV) and 'I have learnt to be satisfied with what I have . . . I have learnt this secret, so that anywhere, at any time, I am content . . . I have the strength to face all conditions by the power that Christ gives me' (Phil. 4:11–13, GNB).

Little David, when he was lost in Marks & Spencer's, had run frantically all over the store trying to find his source of security. He had worn himself out with his fear, anger and despair, just as we all did when our 'teapots' broke. As David searched the shop, he must have asked himself why his father would let a thing like this happen to him – just as we too have asked questions – but everything would have seemed irrelevant when he finally felt those strong arms holding him tightly and he had completely abandoned himself to his father's love.

So this is the last square on the board. For me, abandonment is finally realising that God himself is the answer to all my basic needs, and trusting myself to him entirely, just as little David relaxed in his father's arms and rested in his love. It is also acceptance, because when we know how God feels about us we can happily accept ourselves, accept other people, and accept life in whatever package it

* Amy Carmichael

may come. 'Oh, how kind our Lord was, for he showed me how to trust him and become full of the love of Christ Jesus' (1 Tim 1.14, LB).


## A Prayer

*'Come to me all you who are broken and need to be mended . . . for "you will have life! I will . . . give you the blessings I promised".'* (Isa. 55:2–3, GNB)

Lord Jesus, I think I am beginning to know you a little better through all that I have been suffering, and still must suffer, because in a small way I can appreciate what you went through for me. Yet all that was in the past, and it might feel a bit far removed from my life here in the present if I was not able to share my own suffering with you and allow you to come into the heart of it with me. This has helped me to feel you close to me here and now, at this present moment.

I admit my life has been broken: my dreams, my hopes, the person I used to be, and the relationships I used to value, all lay in pieces around me. Gradually, one by one I have been giving up all those shattered fragments, together with the grudges and the fears, the sorrow and the pain. Please take my life, broken as it is; I give it to you now as a sacrifice as you gave your life, 'your body broken as a sacrifice for me'.

Help me to live in the difficult circumstances of my life, as you would, and I know that each time I react to people and problems in the way that you would react I shall become a little more like you. Please help my faith not to fail until the day I see you face to face, because the ecstasy of that moment will make everything I have endured totally worthwhile.

'Now we live in the hope of eternal life because Christ rose again from the dead . . . So be truly glad! There is wonderful joy ahead, even though the going is rough for a while down here. These trials are only to test your faith, to see whether or not it is strong and pure . . . your faith is far more precious to God than mere gold. So if your faith remains strong after being tried in the test tube of fiery trials, it will bring you much praise and glory and honour on the day of his return.' (1 Pet. 1:3–7, LB)

# 11

## THE PRACTICAL SIDE OF FORGIVING

Jesus said tantalisingly little about many things, but he left us in no doubt as to how we should cope with the relationships we find 'difficult', and how we should treat the people who cause us misery and pain.

He says we must:

- Forgive them (Matt. 6:14)
- Pray for them (Matt. 5:44)
- Love them (Luke 6:27)
- Not fight back (Matt. 5:39), but do good to them instead (Luke 6:28–29)
- Go to them, and attempt to mend the relationship (Matt. 18:15–17)

Before we go any further, there are two things we should know about these rules:

1. They are impossible without Jesus' help.
2. They are not simply 'nice little suggestions'; instead, they are vital for our eternal well-being. Jesus tells us that on the final Day of Judgement we shall each be treated by God as we have treated others during our lifetime (Luke 6:37 38; Matt. 25:31 46). So if we refuse to forgive, he cannot forgive us (Matt. 6:14).

*One should never mention the words 'forgive' and 'forget' in the same breath. No, we will remember, but in forgiving we no longer use the memory against others.* (Helmut Thielicke, a German pastor who endured the darkest days of the Nazi Third Reich)

## 1. First, Jesus Tells Us We Must Forgive Them

For many people, the lengthy process of forgiving the 'Jesus way' begins the moment we ask him into the centre of our pain to melt away the hard core of anger that has collected there. He then begins to make us both willing and able to forgive. There is often a specific moment when we make the decision to forgive, and to leave behind us at his cross all the resentment and the grudges we have been carrying. This decision is simply an act of the *will*, and it has nothing to do with *feelings*.

This moment of 'releasing forgiveness' becomes more real to some people if they speak out loud, as if they were addressing the person who has hurt them. They say something like this, 'I forgive you for all you have done to hurt me and I cease to blame you for anything and everything.' Many also find it a help to write out a list of all the ways in which they feel they have been hurt, and then to burn the list, or destroy it in some other way.

### *But surely I should wait until the person begins to change?*

Jesus didn't wait until we were sorry. 'It was while we were still sinners that Christ died for us!' (Rom. 5:8, GNB.) He poured out his forgiving grace before we asked for it. Like a beautiful meal laid out before a starving person, all the benefits of Jesus' forgiveness lie there ready – regardless of whether that person refuses the food or sits down and eats it. Our response to the forgiveness that Jesus offers makes no difference to the way he feels about us.

Jesus also told us to love our enemies, not our ex-enemies – in other words, to love them while they are still deliberately hurting us and appearing to have no idea of the pain they are inflicting. Jesus practised this precept as the soldiers hammered the nails into his hands; he did not wait for them to repent first.

### *But surely forgiveness is a two-way transaction?*

To be complete, it is, but at first forgiving is all about what happens in our own hearts; it is between us and God, and the other person

---

*How long must I wrestle with my thoughts and every day have sorrow in my heart?* (Ps. 13:2, NIV)

does not come into it until later. So the method of releasing forgiveness I have just mentioned is equally effective regardless of whether the person who has wronged you is alive or dead.

### But my 'enemy' keeps on thinking up new ways to harm me

Jesus forgave unconditionally. It was not a case of, 'I'll forgive you on condition that you never step out of line again.'

### But I don't feel forgiving – I keep having such angry thoughts

A lot of people think they have failed to forgive because they do not *feel* any different after they have made the decision. A few days later, we could be washing up, sitting in church, or rushing to work when we suddenly think, 'But how *could* he have done that to me?' All the old pain comes flooding back again, and a little voice says, 'You've failed again. You'll never manage to forgive! You've been hurt too much.' Forgiving, though, is not something we do just once; C. S. Lewis suggests that when Jesus said we had to forgive seventy times seven, he was not putting a limit on how many different things we must forgive, but how many times we need to forgive the same sin. We have to keep on and on forgiving the same thing until the pain of the offence, and the memory of the moment, is diminished in our minds to the point where it no longer hurts.

These recurring thoughts of resentment are the little poisonous darts that Satan aims at our minds, and we need to be prepared for them. Every morning when you wake:

- Ask the Holy Spirit to fill you once again with the love and forgiving grace of Jesus.
- Ask for the protection of the blood of Jesus over you for that day.
- Put on your spiritual armour. 'Your strength must come from the Lord's mighty power within you. Put on all of God's armor so that you will be able to stand safe against all strategies and tricks of Satan' (Eph. 6:10–11, LB). This is the prayer I often use:

---

*We take captive every thought to make it obedient to Christ.* (2 Cor. 10:5, NIV)

---

Lord, I put on my helmet of salvation to protect my mind from attack.

The breast plate of righteousness to protect my heart from bitterness.

The belt of truth so that I do not see situations and people wrongly or get things out of proportion.

The iron-studded shoes of a Roman soldier, so I will not slip and slide back in the thought battles of today.

I pick up my shield of faith as I declare that I trust your ability to help me keep on forgiving today.

May I wield my sword effectively and use words of Scripture to defeat Satan as you did.

Please bring the right verses to my mind as I need them.

### *Remember the 'spit out, breathe in' routine*

Whenever a bitter thought 'hits' you throughout the day, 'spit it out' instantly and 'breathe in' the forgiving love of Jesus. The thought itself is not a sin, but welcoming it and sucking it like a toffee is.

It is not the memory you are spitting out (forgiving does not mean forgetting); it is the anger generated by the memory that must be instantly rejected.

### *Use prayer as a weapon*

One of the reasons for linking fasting with prayer is surely because the unpleasant hunger pangs remind us to pray. If every time Satan throws one of these thought missiles at us we use it as a trigger to pray for something or someone, he will soon stop this form of attack because he loathes us to pray. (It is probably better to pray for someone quite unconnected with the painful situation – because that has the same effect as 'thinking about something else' while the nurse gives you the injection!)

Praying in tongues also helps some people.

---

*'No weapon forged against you will prevail and you will refute every tongue that accuses you. This is the heritage of the servants of the Lord, and this is their vindication from me,' declares the Lord.* (Isa. 54:17, NIV)

---

### Singing as a weapon

Another good way to fight bitter thoughts is to sing a praise song or hymn – Satan hates praise. You can easily do it under your breath if you happen to be out shopping, but playing a praise tape in the car or kitchen is much easier!

### Saying the name of Jesus

That name is the most powerful name in the universe, and Satan hates the sound of it more than anything else. So when these 'thought attacks' are at their height, repeating the name of Jesus is a wonderful protection.

### Keep handing over the griefs and sorrows

When the bad memories threaten to overwhelm you, picture the cross of Christ between you and the person who hurt you. Keep reminding yourself that Jesus *was* there with you when all those things were happening. He felt the pain and the insults. He wants to carry all your 'griefs and sorrows', so make a conscious decision to shift them on to him every time your 'memory video' reruns. This is done by telling him how you feel, and asking for his healing. Holding on to the hurts might feel comforting, but it is a sure way of falling into self-pity – and Satan loves setting that trap for us.

### Keep a journey log book

Because the journey of forgiveness takes a long time, it helps many people to record their thoughts and feelings in a note book. Putting anger into words and then writing them down in private is a good way of getting it all out of our systems without the risk of hurting anyone else. It is also helpful to record the positive things, such as verses or sayings, moments when God seemed very close, dreams, or advice from other people. These special things can so easily be forgotten, and during the bad times it helps a lot to look back at them.

---

*In the shelter of your presence you hide them from the intrigues of men; in your dwelling you keep them safe from the strife of tongues.* (Ps. 31:20, NIV)

---

## 2. Jesus Tells Us to Pray for Our Enemies

Perhaps Jesus is best known for saying 'love your enemies', but we all know that's quite impossible! Fortunately, he also told us to pray for them – and we need to do that first because only prayer makes the love possible.

Praying for the person who has hurt us badly is usually the very last thing we want to do; cursing them would be far more natural, but that is exactly how the servants of Satan deal with their enemies. They curse them, bind them with spells and incantations, and do things to harm them, either directly or by sticking pins in effigies made of wax or clay. By commanding us to 'bless those who curse you, pray for those who ill-treat you . . . and do good to them' (Luke 6:28, 35, NIV), Jesus is telling us to treat our enemies in exactly the opposite way.

Praying for the person who has hurt us simply means bringing that person into God's presence and standing side by side before the cross. Sometimes it is easier not to use words at all. Peggy, a friend of mine, has a little stone she picked up on the seashore, which represents to her the person who hurt her so badly. Every morning she holds it out on the palm of her hand. As she exposes her enemy to the love of the Lord, her own heart is also open to that love, and she is finding that all her hatred and bitterness is gradually melting away.

Most of us, however, find 'wordless prayer' very hard. We want to say, 'Lord, change this person – he is sinning badly. Chasten him – and do it soon and hard!' The satisfying mental picture of him writhing in repentance, sobbing in his sack cloth, is quite pleasing – until we realise it is not quite what Jesus meant! He asks us to 'bless' by our prayers, and that means asking God to do good things for him.

Strangely, our prayers do not always change our enemy, but they always change us! Sister Basilea Schlink, when writing about a difficult relationship she had once, says this: 'One day in my distress I prayed fervently, then all of a sudden it was as if the finger of God was pointing not at the other person who was causing me such

> *Lord, stand between him and me. Absorb all the anger that is passing between us. Filter all our feelings through the mesh of your love. You are not bound by a human body so you can hold me in your arms at the same time as you hold him.* (Cath Isaaks)

distress, but at me, "You are the one who has to change".' Perhaps as we pray for our 'enemies', we are reminded of two things that Jesus tells us *not* to do for them: 'Do not judge . . . do not condemn' (Luke 6:37, NIV). Gradually, we begin to see our own part in the painful scenario, and we wonder if it was really all the other person's fault after all. Perhaps we also did or said things that hurt the other person, and although his or her attack on us was wrong, perhaps in some ways we did 'bring it on ourselves'. So praying opens our eyes to our own need of repentance and forgiveness.

### Prayer then begins to help us see the enemy in a new way

It helps to dissolve some of our self-absorption, and we begin to under-stand *why* 'our enemy' might have acted as he did. One day, as Peggy was holding her little stone before God, she 'saw' a vivid picture of a small boy crying beside an empty double bed. She later discovered that her 'enemy' had lost both his parents when he was eight, and this softened her attitude towards him. Prayer does far more than simply make us feel more sympathetic; it takes us right inside our enemy's skin in order to see things through his eyes, think through his mind, and feel through his emotion. Understanding on this level makes 'loving' much easier.

### Praying helps the good memories to surface

Libby felt her childhood had been overshadowed by her father's terrible rages and frequent bouts of depression. 'All my memories of him were bad,' she said, 'until someone suggested that I prayed for him. Then suddenly, I remembered a lovely day we spent in a swimming pool when we had once been on holiday. He had taught me to swim by holding on to me with arms that felt so big and strong. I would have been about eight, and it must have been during one of his good spells, but I was able to thank the Lord for that one good memory – and in time I began to remember other little things too.'

> *Words may only add to the shame and pain, but a gentle act of forgiveness and acceptance can mean so much more . . . a hand clasp can mean, 'I need your love and respect you, you are important to me.'* (David Augsburger)

### Warning!

Understanding your enemy, though, does not mean excusing what he or she has done. Excusing can make forgiveness unnecessary, and is a form of denial. It is wrong to try and make ourselves think, 'He couldn't really help it.' He *could* help it, and trying to 'make allowances for him' is not placing the blame at the cross, so we are in danger of subconsciously holding on to it instead.

### Prayer means showing mercy

The Greek word that we translate into *forgiveness*, which was in everyday use in New Testament times, could equally well have described someone being 'let off' a debt that they owed. So forgiving means stepping away from our natural desire to punish our enemy, and handing him over to God to punish for us. We do not find that too hard to do when we read in the Psalms of the terrible wrath of God that awaits those who hurt the people who belong to him. Then we suddenly realise that the Psalms were written before Jesus showed men what forgiving really means. He said, 'Blessed are the merciful, for they shall obtain mercy,' and the greatest way we can ever show mercy to our enemies is by asking God to stay his wrath and vengeance, and to let them off all that they rightly deserve. This is more than just praying good things for them in this life – it is asking for good things for them in the next life as well! The hottest and deepest part of hell itself would surely be too good for those soldiers who heartlessly nailed the 'hands that flung stars into space' to a cross of wood. Yet Jesus was making room for them in heaven when he asked his Father to forgive them. Stephen had reached the same depth of love when he prayed, 'Lord, lay not this sin to their charge', as his persecutors stoned him to death. We know his prayer was answered, because one of them later became St Paul!

When we first bring 'our enemy' to the foot of the cross, we tend to look down on him from a lofty height as we say grandly, 'Lord, this poor wretch needs your forgiveness, and he certainly needs mine too.' However, as we stand there in the Lord's presence we begin to realise we are not 'looking down at our enemy' any longer, but we are standing right next to him. Still we instinctively say, 'Lord, I'm right, he's wrong. Compared to him, I'm a saint!' Then we look up into the face of Jesus and suddenly we stop comparing ourselves with our enemy, and we begin to see what we really are – worthless, wretched and vile. Our enemy may always have had a low opinion of us, but he has never even begun to see what we are really like! In horror, we realise that the lies he told about us were *kind* in comparison to the truth he could have told – had he known us as Jesus knows us. The cruel things he or she did were only a fraction of all that we deserved.

As we stand there sweating with relief at his ignorance, we suddenly realise that Jesus is not ignorant! He knows the very worst about us, yet he chooses to pour down on us a continuous cascade of love, grace and mercy. As we realise the extraordinary extent of the forgiveness he offers to us, our attitude towards the enemy beside us changes. For once we are united, because in the light of God's holiness we are in the same hopeless state, both totally unworthy of forgiveness, either from God or each other. Yet his unstinting mercy is there for us both. After a real experience of God's love and grace, forgiveness is no longer a grudging 'ought', and it becomes easy. All we do is turn in imagination to our enemy beside us and simply allow the torrent that has flooded into us to flow on and out to him, just as if we were merely an empty pipe – a channel of God's grace, unblocked at both ends. Whether he chooses to receive it is not our problem; it is his. We, though, have been obedient to another command of our master, 'Be merciful, just as your Father is merciful' (Luke 6:36, NIV).

### 3. Jesus Tells Us to Love Them

If we are honest, most of us think that is really asking a bit too much! Why should we be commanded to love someone who causes us nothing but misery? However, we need to remember that God's goal is to make us like himself, and he shows constant benevolence to bad people in the same way that he does to the good. The sun shines just the same on the fields of the churchgoing farmer and his Satanist neighbour.

It does help a little to know that Jesus did not tell us to *feel* loving – just to love. Had he meant the kind of love that is full of passionate feelings, he would have used the Greek word *eros*. If he had wanted us to love our enemy with all the emotional tenderness we reserve for our families, he would have used the word *storge*. He might have used *philia* if he wanted us to feel for our enemies the same kind of deep affection we have for our very dearest friends. However, the word Jesus selected was *agape*, which is not a feeling or an emotion as much as an act of the will. It is a decision to love someone. As William Barclay writes in *The Daily Study Bible*, 'No matter what he does to us, no matter how he treats us, no matter if he insults us or injures us or grieves us, we will never allow any bitterness against him to invade our hearts, but will regard him with that unconquerable benevolence and good will which will seek nothing but his highest good.'

Hate wants to harm and destroy; love desires another's highest good and happiness. If we simply spat out the hate, we should be left with a vacuum – that is why we breathe in the love of Jesus, so that it can flow back out again from us in place of the hate. Love is a move towards a person to do good to them in any possible way.

The idea of acting in a loving way without first *feeling* love is difficult. I was once part of a housegroup for new Christians, one of whom was Shirley. One day she told the group she had never been able to forgive the 'other woman' who had broken up her parents' marriage and destroyed her childhood security. Now, years later, she had still never allowed her father's second wife 'to step over her doorstep'.

'I suppose now I'm a Christian I'm going to have to forgive her and even try and love her too,' she added. A few days later she called on me in a panic. Her father had just rung to say he and his wife were in the district and wanted to drop in for a cup of tea.

'How do I treat her?' she demanded.

'You welcome her into your home and treat her with love,' I replied.

'But I don't *feel* loving yet,' she said.

'*Act as if* you loved her,' I said, and explained Pascal's little phrase that had helped me so much with depression and doubt, and added Selwyn Hughes's maxim, 'You can act yourself into feelings even if you cannot feel your self into actions.' 'Loving actions come before loving feelings and not the other way about,' I added.

'It worked!' she told me a few hours later. 'I hated her as I answered the doorbell, but then made myself switch on the love of Jesus and pretended like mad. I felt a fraud at first, but by the time they left I caught myself thinking, "Dad did all right for himself in the end – she's really rather a nice person after all." We have promised to keep in touch from now on, and I haven't felt so close to my dad for years.'

### 'Love always protects'

The NIV rendering of 1 Corinthians 13:7 is 'love . . . always protects'. One of the most valuable things we possess is our reputation. We would never dream of destroying our enemy's car or house, yet by defending our own reputation we automatically destroy his. When sympathetic friends want to hear 'our side of the story', the only way we can put ourselves in a good light is by putting him in a correspondingly bad light. By pointing out to others all his sins and failings, we alter the way they think of him in the future. If we make his shortcomings the topic of conversation over a cup of coffee or glass of beer or make him the butt of our witty little jokes, we are demolishing him publicly. If we 'produce' him as a prayer topic, and sadly shake our heads over his 'lack of spirituality', we are not protecting him, and so we are not loving him. Everything we say about another Christian behind his back should build him up in the eyes of our hearers. Jesus tells us clearly that we should talk to our enemy about his faults face-to-face in private (Matt. 18:15). Of course, we can safely talk about him to Jesus himself, but we must be careful how we talk to other people.

### 4. Jesus Says, 'Do Not Fight Back – Instead, Do Good to Your Enemies'

Forgiving is hardest of all for those who live with their 'enemy', and have to face daily insults and humiliation. It is also difficult for those who feel that their enemy is continually working against them to harm them or those they love. In such cases, forgiveness becomes an active and daily experience. So what does Jesus tell us to do about that?

Most people the world over know that Jesus said, 'If someone smites you on the right cheek, turn to him the left cheek also.' Now the only way that the average right-handed man could hit a man like that is by using the back of his hand. In the days when Jesus said this, to hit a Jew in that way was twice as insulting as using the palm of the hand. So Jesus is saying, 'Even if someone offers you the worse possible insult, do not retaliate.'

However, Jesus did not mean us to stand by passively while someone hurts us over and over again. To do that would simply be to allow all the pain to flow into a vacuum. So he also tells us to 'do good to those who hate you'. In other words, 'don't just stand there while he hits you, do something active – pay back the evil he does to you by doing something good to him in return'. Jesus himself did this the night a mob came to arrest him. Peter jumped to his defence and slashed off the ear of one of the men, but Jesus healed him instantly. 'If your enemy is hungry, feed him; if he is thirsty, give him something to drink . . . Do not be overcome by evil, but overcome evil with good' (Rom. 12:20–21, NIV). When Abraham Lincoln was criticised for being 'kind' to his enemies instead of destroying them, he said, 'Do I not destroy my enemies when I make them my friends.'

James, the minister of a large church, had a terrible time when his congregation began to split because of a power struggle. He made a promise to the Lord that every time he heard on the 'grapevine' of some new criticism hurled at him, or a fresh lie being circulated, that he would do some definite act of kindness for the person concerned. 'Sometimes it was only giving them a smile or a wave across the street, or simply a prayer for God's blessing in some specific way,' he told us. 'But it kept my heart sweet and helped me through those horrible months. In the end the trouble all died down, and the Lord's name was not dishonoured by the disintegration of our church community.'


## Not Fighting Back Means Giving Up Our Right to Be Vindicated

Suppose your enemy threatened to destroy your Christian ministry or rob you of your role in life, or your job, by telling lies about you behind your back, or even accusing you falsely to your face. What about fighting back then? As a human being your first reaction would probably be to justify yourself in the eyes of other people, by speaking out in your own defence or by taking legal action. After all, telling lies about people is defamation of character and the person surely ought to be sued for that? Yet forgiving the 'Jesus way' means giving up our right to be vindicated. He said in Matthew 5:40 (NIV): 'If someone wants to sue you and take your tunic, let him have your cloak as well.' The average Jew in those days might well have two or three 'tunics', but only one cloak. It was really a thick outer garment that he wore as a robe in the day, but used as a blanket at night. The law said a man's tunic could be taken as a pledge, but never his cloak – legally, that had to be handed back by sunset. Jesus is challenging here our natural instinct to stand up for our rights. St Paul also condemns disputes, battles and lawsuits among Christians in 1 Corinthians 6:1–6, and then he goes on to say that such things are a sign of defeat: 'Why not rather be wronged? Why not rather be cheated? Instead, you yourselves cheat and do wrong, and you do this to your brothers!' (vv. 7–8, NIV.)

'But surely Christians are in the world to be salt and light, so we must right wrongs and fight injustice!' you may think. Yes, we must, so long as we only 'right the wrongs' done to other people. We must be very careful how we fight injustice when we personally are the victim, because that is not following the example of Jesus who: 'remained silent and gave no answer' when lying accusations were being hurled at him (Mark 14:57–61; Isa. 53:7).

A friend of ours was involved recently in an extremely painful power struggle within a Christian organisation. He made a definite attempt to mend the relationship between himself and his main antagonist, but the other man simply would not respond. Here is part of a letter in which our friend described to us his feelings:

> I felt desperately disappointed when the reconciliation failed, until I realised it was the loss of my reputation and status that was mostly upsetting me. I had hoped that the reconciliation would manipulate him into repairing the ruins of my life, but I saw that if I forgave him it meant leaving all the chaos he had caused in God's hands. I would have to stop working to clear my name, and turn my back on the mess and deliberately walk away. I risked never being exonerated, but I decided that personal justice was not as important to me as the peace with God that I knew I would receive when I forgave.

### Burning the evidence

Marie had been all knotted up inside by bitterness ever since she had been dismissed from her position as 'matron' of a local government home for the elderly. She believed it was because she had been unfairly accused by a member of her staff, and she also felt she had been badly treated by the 'powers that be' in the DSS. For some years, she had kept all kinds of letters and documents stored in her attic, 'just in case' she could one day use them to have herself reinstated.

During a week's retreat in a healing centre, she began to long to be free from all the resentment and anger that had long been causing her many physical and emotional problems. Even with the help of skilled counsellors, she simply could not seem to release it all, and in the end it was felt that there was some kind of block preventing her inner healing. On the last day of her stay, she suddenly remembered the trunk full of correspondence in her attic. 'But I can't get rid of all that,' she protested, when her counsellors told her to go home and burn it. 'It's my last hope of ever getting my rights.'

'Which is more important to you, your rights or your health and peace?' was the challenge with which they sent her home. As she walked in through her front door, she still had not decided what she would do, but by the following evening she 'made the biggest bonfire ever' in her back garden and finally gave up her chance of vindication.

When she told me that story a few months ago, I had already begun to write this book, but all the inspiration had petered out after the first two chapters. I had put the book on the 'back burner', thinking perhaps it was not what God wanted me to do after all. Then when Marie told me about her attic trunk, I remembered a file full of letters and documents I had also put away. They concerned some personal criticism that I had felt was untrue, and I had collected all kinds of material – thinking that one day I might be able to use it to clear my name. Within days of making my own bonfire, the ideas for the book were positively pouring into my computer! Fancy expecting God to help me write a book on forgiveness with all that in my own filing cabinet!

## *Warning!*

Not fighting back does not mean denying natural anger. You *will* feel angry – often! So do turn back to Chapter 9 on anger, and deal with it by the method suggested there.

### *Surely Jesus does not expect us to let ourselves be doormats?*

Jesus told us in Matthew 5:41 (NIV): 'If someone forces you to go one mile, go with him two miles.' He said that to people who lived in an occupied land. Romans could compel someone to be their porter or guide by legal right, and this is what happened to Simon of Cyrene when he was ordered to carry the cross for Jesus that first Good Friday. Perhaps what Jesus meant is that when someone makes unreasonable demands on us, we should do twice as much as they ask, and do it cheerfully and without resentment. He also pointed out (Matt.20:28) that he had come to serve others and give his life for them, not to stand on his right to be served himself.

It is *not* loving to allow a person to become a tyrant and walk all over our human dignity, because that is not good for them. Yet how can we prevent them doing this if we are not to insist on our rights? This is a dilemma that has to be decided in each individual situation; however, it is worth remembering that people always tend to value us as much as we privately value ourselves. Someone who 'walks tall', looks people right in the eye, takes care of their appearance, and holds their head high is usually treated with automatic respect without having to insist upon it. We need to keep on reminding ourselves in situations where we are likely to be put down and despised that we are *not* worthless, useless stooges; we are princes or princesses of heaven, valued highly by God himself, who says we are honoured in his sight (Isa. 43:4). Here again, Pascal's words 'act as if' might be helpful.

### 5. Jesus Tells Us to Go to Him

Mending broken relationships is of paramount importance to Jesus, and it was the reason he came to earth in the first place. He wanted to make a reconciliation between men and God, and he was willing to give his life to make this possible. So it is not surprising that he cares so deeply about our broken relationships, and he makes it clear that forgiveness not only happens inside our hearts, but is also about reaching out to restore contact. Three times when talking about people who hurt us, he uses the same four words, 'go to your brother':

- 'If your brother has a grievance against you, go to him' (Matt. 5:23 paraphrased)
- 'If you have something against your brother, go to him' (Matt. 18:15 paraphrased)
- 'If your brother sins, go to him and confront him' (Luke 17:3 paraphrased)

To say, 'I have forgiven him, but I prefer to keep out of his way,' is not real forgiveness, and it also robs us of all the blessings that forgiveness brings. It can be extremely embarrassing, or even terrifying, to 'go to your brother', but of course reconciliation cost Jesus an awful lot too!

I have often heard people say that when they asked the Lord to show them how and when to make a reconciliation, he arranged it all for them at just the right moment.

Peggy, the friend I mentioned earlier who prayed for her 'enemy' by using a stone to represent him, was most perplexed about how she could make some kind of contact with the hospital consultant who had been so harsh and unkind to her, and whose mismanagement of her treatment had left her crippled and in constant pain. 'I did ring and try to make an appointment, but he would not see me. I thought about trying to find out where he lived and ringing on the doorbell one day, but I feel that "an Englishman's home is his castle", and that that would be unfair. So in the end I prayed that if the Lord wanted us to meet, he would arrange it for me.

'About a year later, I was out shopping when I met him in the street. He didn't recognise me, but I went up to him and shook his hand, saying, "You probably don't remember me, but you looked after me in hospital five years ago, and I would like you to know I'm getting better all the time." He smiled and looked genuinely pleased as we said goodbye. That was all that happened, and I don't think it would have been right to say "I forgive you for all your negligence and for being so vile to me," because that would just have been dumping my negative feelings on him. Surely forgiveness can be just a smile and a handshake?' I am sure Peggy is right, and that releasing forgiving through words can sometimes cause serious damage.

Gayle was forty-two before she allowed herself to remember that her father sexually abused her on a number of occasions while her mother was present. She needed months of help from a counsellor, her doctor and vicar before she was able to face up to what had happened. When she felt she had forgiven in her own heart she decided to go and see her parents, something she had not done for some years. Against all advice, she expressed her forgiveness to them in words. Her parents were horrified, and told her that she had made it all up. Obviously they were afraid that she would make it public and that her father's reputation as a church leader would be ruined, so they wrote to the three people who had been helping their daughter and denied the whole thing vehemently. 'She was always a very deceitful and difficult child,' was how they described her. The poor girl was devastated; it was her word against theirs, and their angry reaction almost finished her attempt to forgive. Had she expressed her forgiveness by being good to her parents and offering them her company as they grew older, things might have ended very differently.

*But suppose all the old feelings come back when I see him again?*

This is exactly what happened to Corrie ten Boom. She and her sister Betsie had been prisoners in Ravensbrück concentration camp, and Betsie eventually died there. After the war, Corrie travelled all over the world speaking about the power of forgiveness, but one day when she was in Germany a man came up to her at the end of a church service. She recognised him as one of the worst of the Nazi guards at the camp, and his cruel treatment had caused her sister terrible suffering. All the memories came pouring back as she looked into his face, but he did not recognise her as he came up holding out his hand.

'I have recently become a Christian,' he said, 'and I want to ask your forgiveness for the things prisoners like you had to suffer in the war.' Corrie stood frozen, quite unable to reach out and take the hand that he was offering to her. Then she prayed, 'Lord, let your forgiveness flow through me to this man, and help me to see him as you see him now.' As she forced herself to take his hand, she felt love and forgiveness flowing through her and she was able to greet him with genuine warmth.

### When we go to our enemy, we are not:

- Attempting to make him aware of how much he has hurt us so that he will feel guilty and ask for *our* forgiveness.
- Trying to justify ourselves or putting our own point of view.
- Trying to change his heart and stop him from doing any more damage.
- Trying to be spiritually 'one up' on him.
- Overcoming fear, in the same way that someone who is terrified of snakes might force themselves to visit the reptile house at the zoo.
- Expressing anger in a restrained way by telling the 'enemy' how we feel.
- Making a grand gesture of forgiveness; instead, we must humbly offer it and also ask forgiveness for any pain that we may have caused through our words, actions or attitudes of criticism, resentment or lack of love.

'Going to our brother' is simply an outward and visible sign of an inward and spiritual grace. We have let go and forgiven in our hearts – privately. When we 'go to our brother', it means putting the thoughts and feelings into actions. Some people find it easier to use actions rather than words, others feel the need to talk at depth – either on the first occasion or later. It really does not matter exactly what happens; the important thing is the new relationship of friendship and trust that emerges from the meeting.

### What if they do not respond?

Forgiveness is difficult enough when it is mutual, but it really gets tough after we have dared to make an attempt at reconciliation only to have our efforts flung back in our faces with a few more insults added to the pile we are already trying to forgive! In Matthew 18:16, Jesus tells us what to do in that event: 'But if he will not listen to you, take one or two other persons with you . . .' (GNB). It is always a help to get another perspective on a difficult situation, and I am sure that Jesus means this 'third party' to be a mutual friend rather than a couple of 'heavies' taken along to frighten 'the enemy' into submission! Perhaps in present-day terms, the equivalent would be counsellors or other wise people who will pray about the situation, as well as giving advice and attempting to keep the peace.

If that step fails, Jesus tells us to take the matter to the group of believers to whom you belong. Of course, not even bishops, moderators or housechurch leaders can *make* someone else forgive, but surely the value of bringing in all this spiritual 'muscle power' is to battle with Satan through prayer. Hudson Taylor tells us that, 'Men can be moved for God by prayer alone,' but sadly, when a relationship between two Christians breaks down, the church can be so busy gossiping and taking sides that a general punch-up is more likely than a prayer meeting!

Finally, Jesus says something that at first sounds rather strange: 'If he refuses to listen even to the church, treat him as you would a pagan or a tax collector' (Matt. 18:17, NIV). Some people take that to mean we are to wash our hands of the person, and exclude him or her for ever from our lives; however, that is *not* how Jesus treated tax collectors. Matthew himself was a tax collector until the uncondemning love of Jesus won his heart.

Surely Jesus is saying, 'When you have done everything you can by active means to restore peace, then simply go on treating the person in the way I treated the unlovable, with the kind of love that is willing to go on waiting and never gives up hope.'

There is always a sense of deep regret and even rejection, but just because your 'enemy' will not forgive does not mean that your own journey of forgiveness is incomplete. It is a comfort to know that Jesus understands this kind of sadness only too well, having his offer of forgiveness turned down is something that happens to him constantly; however, it never makes him stop being willing to forgive. Surely, through this passage in Matthew 18, he makes it clear that we should not go on 'pestering' by further contacts, but there never comes a time when you exclude an unrepentant person from your heart.

## *Mending marriages*

Sometimes the most difficult 'enemy' to forgive is the one to whom you were once married. Perhaps it's because love and hate are so closely linked, but some people find it hard to forgive fully after a marriage break-up because they feel that the only possible outcome of forgiveness is getting back together again. When both partners are willing to forgive, this is often the 'happy ever after ending', but for many reasons it is not always possible. Obviously it is not within the scope of a book like this to advise on anything so complicated, but the fact remains that forgiving from the heart is vital – whether such reconciliation means a second honeymoon, or simply the ability to communicate again in a peaceful and friendly manner.

## But what if the person we need to forgive is already dead?

Some people think that this makes forgiving impossible, but that is definitely not the case. Forgiveness must still be expressed either by words spoken out loud, or by some kind of concrete action. Some people write a letter to the person who hurt them, describing the incident in detail, and this helps them to live the experience again and bring their reactions to the surface for confession and healing. Forgiveness can then be offered on paper as part of the letter, or spoken out loud before a witness. Forgiveness should also be requested for any hatred and grudge-bearing involved. Some people take the letter to a place associated with the dead person and, if possible, bury or burn it there. They can then finally relinquish the person to God in a prayer.

## The end of the forgiveness journey

Forgiving is so close to the heart of Jesus and he positively lavishes blessing on anyone who perseveres with it to the end. Surely the climax comes when we begin to see just how much we have gained from all that has happened. In Chapter 3 I described how Joseph's jealous brothers sold him into slavery when he was a child. They meant to harm him, but as he looked back over all those years in Egypt he was finally able to say, 'But God meant it for good.' The people who have helped me write this book have all found forgiving terribly difficult, but they all agree that Jesus was right when he said, 'Happy and to be envied are you when people despise, hate and exclude you on account of the Son of man. Rejoice and be glad at such a time and exult and leap for joy for behold your reward is rich and great and intense and abundant in heaven' (Luke 6:22–23, AMP).

Someone once said to me:

'When we are able to be positively glad about the horridest things Satan hurls at us, they become like boomerangs whizzing back at Satan, who launched them at us in the first place.'

The following words were found scrawled near the body of a dead child in Ravensbrück concentration camp, where 92,000 women and children died:

O Lord, remember those of ill will,
but do not remember all the suffering they inflicted on us,
remember the fruits we have brought, thanks to our suffering,
our comradeships, our loyalty, our generosity,
the greatness of heart which has grown out of all this.

---

## A Final Prayer

Lord, you know how hard I find this process of forgiveness. Sometimes I think I've finally 'let go' and then something triggers off all those old memories and the bitter feelings they generate. Please help me not to give up. Give me your kind of persistence; keep me working at it even if it takes me the rest of my life. Like Paul, make me able to say, 'Forgetting what is behind and straining towards what is ahead, I press on towards the goal to win the prize for which God has called me heavenwards in Christ Jesus' (Phil. 3:13–14, NIV).

Thank you, Lord, for all that you are doing in my life; for all the repairing, reshaping and renewing that is going on inside me. It's painful at times, but I know it will be worth it in the end. Most of all, I thank you that I do not have to go through all this alone. I know you are there beside me all the time and you will never give up on me, whatever happens. Thank you for teaching me that all I need is you, both in this life and the next. Amen.

It says in the Bible: 'Blessed is the man who perseveres under trial, because when he has stood the test, he will receive the crown of life that God has promised to those who love him' (Jas. 1:12, NIV).